MW01625120

WHY ME?
WHY *NOT* ME?

"An uplifting spiritual journey of newfound peace and joy"

SABRINA DODSON HAYES

ISBN 978-1-4958-1296-5

Published August 2017

INFINITY PUBLISHING
1094 New DeHaven Street, Suite 100
West Conshohocken, PA 19428-2713
Toll-free (877) BUY BOOK
Local Phone (610) 941-9999
Fax (610) 941-9959
Info@buybooksontheweb.com
www.buybooksontheweb.com

Contents

Joy Cometh in The Morning (preface) vii
Acknowledgements xi
Introduction xiii

PART 1: **DISCOVERING MY SPIRITUAL ASSIGNMENT** 1
Why I Wrote This Book 3
What Is A Christian Testimony 9

PART 2: **SHARING PERSONAL TESTIMONIES** 11
Who Will Cry For the Little Boy 13
I Won't Complain 31
A Heart to Heart Conversation with God 49
Amazing Grace 65
Beauty Is Only Skin Deep 81

PART 3: **CONCLUSION** 101
Why Me? Why Not Me? 103
Finding Purpose and Joy In Your Life 107

Appendix I: A Tribute to the Lonely 109
Appendix II: Discussion Questions 117

This book is dedicated to my father, Manuel Reese Dodson, Sr. — the only man I've ever known whose word was truly his bond. Daddy, your incorrigible faith, unconditional love and habitual obedience in God's word was always reflective in the life you lived. Through your spiritual guidance and training, I am so grateful to respectfully continue your legacy of unprecedented courage and remarkable strength as I dedicate my life in helping others endure the unexpected trials and tribulations of this world.

You are forever in my thoughts
and in my heart!

Preface

"Weeping May Endure for a Night, but Joy Cometh in the Morning"
Psalms 30:5

When God takes you through something—regardless of *what it is*, don't spend countless, unproductive hours weeping, worrying and wondering why this is happening to you. Instead, cast all your cares on the Lord, set your faith on cruise control and, take the test…endure the challenge…enjoy the peace.

Learning how to maintain your joy in the midst of a storm is undeniably a major undertaking. Whenever a crisis occurs in your life, it's often difficult to know what to do, how to manage and how to recover. Sometimes we find ourselves in unfamiliar territory struggling with the temptation to doubt God's love, goodness, and faithfulness in light of what we are going through.

Your mind may scream questions like, "Why me?", "Why did God let this happen?" or "What did I do to deserve this?" But regardless of how senseless or hopeless a situation may seem—God is merciful. He has a purpose for every difficulty, every trial and every fragment of pain you encounter. God allows things to happen for His reasons, whether or not we understand them. It's important to remember that God's plan is not to destroy you through adversity but to refine you and draw you closer to him—teaching you discipline and obedience.

The Bible speaks about three essential characteristics universally associated with God: Omniscience "the quality of knowing all things at once"; Omnipresence "unlimited presence in every place at the same time"; Omnipotence "all powerful". Simply stated—God *knows* all things, He *sees* all things and He is *everywhere* all the time. He is our Comforter, our Savior, our Redeemer and our Friend. There is absolutely no pit so deep that God won't lift you out of. He can repair your brokenness, restore your wholeness and renew your spirit. And, He will continue to strengthen you and favor you with extraordinary redemption for all that has been lost in your life.

Why Me? Why Not Me? is a book of encouragement and inspiration revealing the marvelous truth of God's supernatural power through the life changing testimonies of persons who have experienced the most unimaginable hardship and misery in their lives. The testament of their remarkable strength and courage lies in their desire to share with others their heartbreaking story and how the agony they endured helped them to gain spiritual insight, confidence and peace.

As each person shares their story—their sole mission is to prayerfully minister to those who are harboring deep embedded hurt, shame, embarrassment or pain. And, bless others with the revelation that personal suffering is merely a catalyst toward hope, deliverance and divine change. These powerful testimonies will uplift you and reveal God's astounding power, grace and love. So when the trials and tribulations of this world violate and infringe upon your life—you can resist the temptation of asking the question, *"Why me?"* but stand firm in your conviction and with bold confidence say....."Why ***Not*** Me?"

Acknowledgements

My heartfelt thanks to….

My wonderful children: Dante, Antaeus and Shannon. Words can't possibly describe how thankful I am to God for blessing me, but most importantly—***trusting*** me to foster, educate and nurture His three precious babies. I couldn't imagine a greater honor. Each day I'm totally amazed and exceptionally pleased at your continuous spiritual growth and development in God's word along with deep-seated morals and such an impressive level of determination in your professional endeavors. Thank you for loving me and taking care of your mama.

My siblings: Manuel Jr., Paulette, Roland Sr., Daniel Sr.—what a special bond we share. Our unconditional love and support for one another was infused in our spirits from the very beginning by incredibly compassionate, encouraging, supportive and loving parents, Manuel and Mary Dodson. We are truly the fortunate ones—blessed with phenomenal parents who were always completely faithful and obedient in God's word and unquestionably determined to ensure we were too. I love you.

To my devoted, sweet and wonderful aunts on my father's side (*the Dodsons & the Hairstons*): Jean Robinson, Deana Walters, Chiquilla Polain and my dearly departed aunts, Bernice Morris and Elsie Dodson. What a unique privilege to be part of two notable families with such a compelling heritage of strength and perseverance. The magnitude of our family far exceeds the thousands yet we share a distinctive unity reflective of our ancestry. Hugs and kisses to you for your continuous guidance, direction and oh my, the "put your foot in it" delectable pound cake, potato salad and all the other scrumptious, mouthwatering food dishes you've prepared for the family over the years.

Uncle John Smith (Jay L.) my mom's baby brother, you encouraged me to write this book, without you even knowing it, by sharing your extraordinary wisdom and spiritual insightfulness—thank you. My Aunt Beatrice (Bea), my mom's baby sister—I love you.

A special thanks to my Sunday Brunch Book Club (SBBC) sisters who are truly my family. You inspire me through your remarkable intellect, discernment, encouragement, spiritual fortitude and authentic love.

And, sincere loving thanks to all of my close friends and coworkers who listened to me and helped me through this journey. Your input was invaluable and your love and prayers will always be greatly appreciated.

Introduction

According to the Guinness Book of World Records, the Oxford English Dictionary is the most comprehensive single-language print dictionary in the world. It is widely regarded as the accepted authority on the English language capturing well over 600,000 words, one million quotations and a wealth of informative phrases and commentaries.

But try finding the right blend of words to say to someone who has just experienced the most gut wrenching tragedy and it's as if our familiarity with the English language becomes surprisingly foreign, leaving us with an unusual state of verbal paralysis. No profound spiritual response. No deep, insightful message. No meaningful discernment. All most of us can think to say at such a difficult time is, "I'm so sorry."

Isn't it amazing how words often escape us when a serious crisis or tragedy occurs? Instead of revealing our natural, distinctive wit to say something comforting, caring and considerate—we have a tendency to become silent, tongue-tied or not quite sure what to say. My guess is that we too are struggling with the horrific shock of the event, trying desperately to make sense of it all and frantically searching to identify that perfect flow of words. It's during these challenging moments that we want so badly to offer words of encouragement and reassurance. But often what we want to say is not always the best or most helpful at that time. Sometimes an overindulgence of words can get misplaced and even misunderstood when people are suffering. Most people are usually so emotionally traumatized by an unexpected misfortune that the kindest of words can't begin to penetrate the surface of their pain. Now, that's not to say that we shouldn't extend our support. People are genuinely receptive toward warm gestures appreciating the thoughtfulness of others. But what's most important, in our pursuit to help others, is to offer them the key essential ingredients for healing—prayer, faith and hope.

Dealing with tragedy, of any kind, is devastatingly difficult and rears its ugly head in various forms. A parent's worst nightmare is to receive that dreadful call in the middle of the night or startled by a knock on the door from a police officer delivering the horrifying news that their child has been killed in an accident, murdered by some demented lunatic or reported missing because they never arrived at school. There are no magic words or miraculous cures that can alleviate the pain of a grieving mother or father who has lost a child. Comforting hugs won't wipe away the sadness of a little girl's hopeless spirit after losing her parents at a very young age. Soothing expressions can't repair the mental and emotional anguish and damage of a young woman who was repeatedly raped by her father during the most innocent and precious years of her life. Gifts and tokens of kindness can't compensate for the promising, lucrative career of a star athlete whose legs were amputated as a result of a serious car accident. A spiritual counselor or therapist can't explain nor erase the devastating memory of a parent trying to fathom why their healthy, vibrant teenager committed suicide.

Tragedy is a very real, uninvited phenomenon that can overwhelm you—catching you totally off guard, unprepared and leaving you numb with fear and trepidation. And regardless of how strong or even how infallible you may think you are—life is incredibly delicate and has the unintentional capacity to be terribly cruel especially when you're faced with the unpredictable catastrophes that can destroy and desecrate your life. Even in spite of one's level of resilience—life crisis are incorrigible creatures causing unnecessary complications, untimely circumstances and horrific obstacles.

Generally speaking, most people are relatively clueless on how grueling and exhausting it is to deal with a tragedy—until it happens to them. Sadly enough there will come a time when everyone will face some terrible ordeal and forced to embrace the reality of how to manage. Some people will become consumed with grief, emotionally frozen, not caring about anyone or anything; Some will become insensitive with their feelings, paralyzed with confusion, not sure what to do or how to do it; Some will desperately try to contend with a myriad of unfamiliar emotions; Some will descend toward a fragile, comatose state of mind, losing their ability to think, act or feel; Some will become angry at God blaming Him for their suffering; Some will give up completely expressing their will to die; Yet, some will remain steadfast and faithful in God's word allowing the holy spirit to resonate and deliver them from that dark place of desperation and depression.

The truth is—none of us are immune from bad things. I honestly believe that most of us could tolerate suffering if we had just the slightest indication as to why it was happening. For instance, a pregnant woman understands that the excruciating, agonizing pains of labor are all part of the delivery process and most importantly—new life. But it's the irrational, unpredictable events that are so perplexing—forcing us to believe that such an awful occurrence had to be triggered by some immoral or indecent act on our part and the consequences of that tragedy is our deserving punishment. But this couldn't be further from the truth because God doesn't work that way. It would be contradictory to God's character to believe this. God can't be good and evil—it goes against His very nature.

Like most, I struggled for years with the baffling question, "Why do bad things happen to good people?" It was so hard for me to understand why the most horrendous things happen to the nicest people. Take the most dreadful example, the death of a child. It may not make a lot of sense in our natural mind why God would allow such an innocent life to end so abruptly. But from God's perspective, that life is not lost. God is able to restore to that child eternal life, so no loss is suffered on the part of the child.

The stories you are about to read are true. They are not fiction. They are not stories made up for emotional appeal. They are miracle stories featuring persons who fought hard to not only deal with their pain but how they spent years trying to mask it from others. Now they travel the road of healing and have been delivered from the mental and emotional bondage so that they can speak freely about the love of Almighty God and how His grace sustained them through the most difficult period in their lives.

As you read the personal testimonies in this book—you may think that the suffering endured by these individuals, in comparison to something you've either directly or indirectly experienced, is not all that bad. But as the younger generation would say, "don't get it twisted". Remember, my pain is not your pain and your test is not my test. And as the wise and sensible older generation would say—we all have our cross to bear.

In spite of what anyone else may think, a tragic ordeal is valid to the one going through it. You may not always understand your test, why God chose you to take it or if you have the wherewithal to endure it. But one thing for sure as you experience life's trials and tribulations—you will begin to know God for yourself and how His power and the power of prayer will begin to resonate within your spirit giving you the strength to press onward toward a place of peace and solitude.

Although the stories are true—the names have been changed to preserve and protect the privacy and respect of those individuals who were courageous enough to share.

John 16:33

"I have said these things to you,
that in me you may have peace.
In the world you will have tribulation.
But take heart; I have overcome the world."

PART 1:

Discovering My Spiritual Assignment

Why I Wrote This Book

Writing this book was by far one of the greatest decisions I've ever made—that's precisely when my own healing began and when God revealed to me that the personal testimonies in this book would not only provide a deep sense of spiritual restoration to those battling an arduous challenge, but a means to educate and encourage others on how to recapture their joy and live a life of peacefulness and contentment. And most notably, to honor and document the difficult experiences of the persons named in this book, who have remarkably weathered the storms of life through an inconceivable, uncanny power of determination, courage and faith.

After spending several months carefully contemplating what *I* thought this book should be about—it was the Holy Spirit who vigilantly guided my vision in how to create the layout; how to delicately construct the personal testimonies; and, how to effectively reveal the riches of God's unconditional love. During this period, I unquestionably sensed, deep within my spirit, a powerful unction that God had a job for me to do. So, in my humble effort to obey God—I did precisely what he had tasked me to do. Well… at least that was my initial objective until I allowed personal and professional endeavors to disrupt my focus, creating an unproductive impact on this most important task.

It's so interesting how we react when God places a divine task within our spirit. Instead of immediately welcoming such a compelling revelation—we sometimes have a tendency to pause, allowing ourselves to either question the task, ignore the calling or resist it all together. Clearly, I didn't ignore nor resist the calling but I did have the audacity to place it on the back burner, telling myself I would get to it as soon as I had the time. I laugh now at my spiritual ignorance. A part of me actually thought I could decide when *I* was ready to begin a spiritual assignment from God. Well, it's not like writing a book has a date of completion stamped on it so I figured I would get to it when I had the time. Apparently, I didn't recognize nor appreciate the revelation that writing this book and sharing my own testimony would afford me the privilege to experience an extraordinary level of insight and awareness from God.

I've always thought of myself as being an overly confident, responsible and self assured person placing heavy emphasis on the things I was required to do in every facet of my life. But for the past couple of years, I'd tirelessly struggled with this unexplainable, heightened sense of duty and desire to do much more than I had been doing. Yet, the irony was that I really felt I had accomplished a lot in my life and in fact—I really believed I had done enough! For over thirty-five years, I'd worked exceptionally hard to achieve all that I had been blessed with but as time passed, I found myself feeling restless, tired and slightly discouraged. Something vital was missing from my life but I just couldn't put my finger on what it was or why I felt so discontent. Did I feel I was ready for retirement at a premier age of 60 even though my bank account said differently? Did I want to stay at home watching movies all day and fumbling around the house? Was I merely feeling the loneliness and void since my children were grown and living their own lives? I really didn't have an answer to these questions. But one thing I was quite sure about—I wasn't the least bit interested in doing anything else that required an enormous amount of mental, emotional or physical energy—I was truly zapped out. Being married for twenty-five years, raising three children and assuming the responsibility of a demanding career—I couldn't take on another thing. I wasn't interested in extracurricular activities (I did enough of that with my kids); people drama (I loathe drama); people problems (I had to stop being an enabler), or voluntarily delving into any bizarre issues (I run from conflict, controversy and the crazies). I just wanted to rest, chill out and allow my life to become status quo—devoting all my free time to myself and doing only what I wanted—*so I thought.*

I must have had a brief period of lunacy. I immediately came to the realization that this mode of thinking was not only selfish but self centered. Here I stand—alive and well, always testifying to others how God has blessed me beyond my wildest imagination, how He has favored me with an abundance of creative gifts and talents and I have the unprecedented gall to feel as if my work is done. Believe me when I tell you that God delivered a message to my spirit—LOUD and CLEAR. He had a different plan for my life and divinely reminded me that a child of God, a devout Christian, a believer's work…is NEVER done. For over a year, through conviction and coaxing from the Holy Spirit, I was finally ready to begin.

Writing a book of this magnitude is a complex task. It requires an enormous level of discipline, research and commitment. While writing, there were so many times my mind would go into a million different directions causing a great deal of anxiety and apprehension. I felt as if my words were all wrong and that the vision and concept I had for the book were just not coming together as I hoped. I found myself becoming slightly disheartened-ready to throw in the towel. But low and behold usually in the early hours of the morning, God would awaken me with the most ingenious ideas. He would bless my spirit with incredible inspiration, fill my mind with the perfect flow of words and provide me with step by step direction and guidance on how to complete this task. As usual, I felt blessed and most of all—thankful. I immediately shook off the self pity, stepped out on faith and placed my mental focus on a positive, constructive track. I prayed for spiritual insight in my writing and in my pursuit to touch the lonely hearts of despair so that this book would be a blessing to all persons searching for change and a new beginning.

This book serves as an inspirational guide for every living person who is a fervent Christian, a pastor, missionary, and for persons who are holding on to unwarranted anger, resentment and disappointment toward God for some unjust tragedy that has occurred in their lives. And, particularly for lost souls who dare to question God or have doubts of His amazing grace and absolute love.

Believers and non-believers, it's time to take a gigantic "Mother May I?" step forward and allow the Holy Spirit and the uplifting messages in this book to manifest within your spirit so you too can experience complete rejuvenation. I did. And now I have a better understanding of the spiritual journey God has planned for my life. I learned two valuable lessons while writing this book—*everyone has a divine purpose and everyone has a testimony.*

What is a Christian Testimony?

It is a personal, powerful and sincere testament of how God has worked a transforming miracle in a person's life through a difficult time or a specific event, (*brokenness, tragedy, severe illness, death, depression)* and what their life was like before they surrendered to God and the difference in their life once they began walking with God.

Many people are uncomfortable sharing their testimony, in spite of the fact that it could serve as a blessing to someone's life. Some are embarrassed, fearful, insecure or too private to disclose the intimate details of their personal experiences. But despite the reasons, every time we share our testimony, our story, we give honor and glory to God giving Him the acknowledgement for what He's done for us. It's through our experiences, our trials and tribulations that our faith is strengthen in Him and how the Holy Spirit continues to dwell within us leading, guiding and shaping us into mature Christians.

Revealing how God delivered you from a hopeless situation is an essential part of ministry. Being an authentic missionary requires us to witness, save souls and serve as a beacon of light, in hope that others will find their way.

PART 2:

Sharing Personal Testimonies

WHO WILL CRY FOR THE LITTLE BOY?

Who will cry for the little boy, lost and all alone?
Who will cry for the little boy, abandoned without his own?
Who will cry for the little boy? Who knows well hurt and pain.
Who will cry for the little boy? He died and died again.
Who will cry for the little boy? A good boy he tried to be.
Who will cry for the little boy, who cries inside of me?"

-Antwone Fisher

Who will cry for the little boy? I will.

My name is Kelvin J. I'm twenty-six years old and I *was* that little boy. No one ever told me that I was born to be hurt. As far back as I can remember I felt sadness and I experienced what seemed like a lifetime of unforgettable pain, intense suffering, disappointment, loneliness, betrayal and an indescribable sense of abandonment from the very people I loved the most and that I thought were placed in my life to love, protect and nurture me. I was wrong.

My dreams of living a happy-go-lucky, carefree life turned nightmare at the pure and precious age of four. My harmless and fragile little spirit had been traumatized, crushed, and shattered beyond recognition by my biological father who repeatedly and brutally beat me, bullied me and sexually abused me practically every night beginning from age four until what should have been the most enjoyable, impressionable age of a young boy's life—thirteen. I remember everything as if it happened yesterday. Every inch of pain, every word he said and how he said it and what was going on around me at the time. You just don't forget horrific, mind blowing ordeals like that no matter how hard you try. And, if another person tells me to get over it and move on—let's just say I hope I'm having a good day.

Like most of you, I'm sure people mean well when they make general clichés—let go of the anger, forgive and forget, time will heal all wounds. But it's so hard to believe these things when you've been through what I have. And, it's even harder to trust the people that say these things because how could they possibly know how you feel. The truth is—only people who have lived through such a dark and dreadful ordeal would know.

The Beginning

At the onset of these vile, degrading sexual encounters—the torture began. My father would strike me so incredibly hard and so viciously with his man sized fist that I actually thought I was going to pass out or worse—die. He dared me to cry, he dared me to whine and he dared me to beg for mercy. In the back of my young innocent mind, I somehow convinced myself that my pitiful, sobbing tears would appeal to his compassionate side and he would choose to stop. I couldn't have been more wrong. Showing any signs of weakness not only caused the beatings to become more severe but gravely provoked his uncontrollable anger—sometimes to an unimaginable level. I just couldn't believe this was happening. What in the world could I have done so wrong that would cause my father, the man chosen as my protector, to harbor such a deep embedded hatred toward me and worse, torment me with every inch of his being.

It was a pleasant, sunny afternoon when the first sexual encounter occurred. My mother was heading out the door for work like she did most evenings around 3:00 pm and before leaving she had given me permission to go outside to watch my cousin and his friends play basketball. I lived in a very small, quiet community where everyone knew everyone. And even back then parents could leave their school age children outside to play without any real concerns or worries. The basketball court couldn't have been more than 500 feet from my house so I sat quietly on the ground, enjoying the game and just happy to be outside around the other kids which didn't happen very often. I was always required to stay in the house and was never allowed to have friends over to play. Within minutes I saw my father charging toward me like an out of control raging bull and what seemed like a traveling speed of 200 miles per hour. He had the most horrid, unsettling look on his face which caused me to become instantly sick at the stomach. The second I was within his reach he yanked me up so hard by my small little arm that I could hear the snap and began to feel the sharp, cringing pain. I really didn't know if my arm was broken or not but needless to say, I was more concerned about what awful act was going to happen once he got me inside our house. One of our neighbors, a very nice middle aged woman witnessed my father's abusive behavior. She told my father that he was terribly wrong and should not be handling a small child in that way. He immediately told her to mind her own F****n business. At this point, I knew he was way over the top and overcome with one of his violent, uncontrollable spells—I'd seen this scary behavior before. So, I did exactly what I was told and scurried into the house.

The moment I stepped foot in that house—I ran into the bathroom. I wanted to quickly get away from my father's view but most importantly, his unnerving ball of fury. I proceeded to wash my hands since they had gotten dirty from sitting on the ground. While I was rinsing my hands, he came into the bathroom, didn't utter a word and grabbed me in the most vicious way punching me in my chest, stomach, and back—over and over again as hard as he could. I think I actually blacked out a couple of times from the excruciating pain. And, I distinctly remember thinking to myself—all of this just because I was playing outside. This sick, demented tactic of beating me was my father's way of keeping me emotionally and mentally paralyzed while he violated or should I say—raped my small, weak and powerless body until I couldn't speak, cry or beg. My father's mission was accomplished—he had me exactly where and how he wanted. I was forced to withstand persecution at the hands of a man I thought loved me and who, by moral and spiritual standards, was authorized to watch over me.

"Daddy, please stop—you're hurting me. I don't like this. Was I bad—is that why you're doing this to me? I want my Mommy. Let me go. Leave me alone. Daddy, please, please stop!"

This was a typical, unheard monologue coming from my faint little voice during those awful sexual intrusions. But the pleading didn't matter to him one bit—he didn't hear me nor did he care. I honestly believe he received immense pleasure from watching me suffer with such agony. And, after each wretched encounter, he never failed to remind me that if I ever revealed to anyone what had happened—he would kill me and cut off my penis. Boy, did he have this picture twisted—it was his penis that needed to be cut off.

On most days, I felt like I was going absolutely crazy. I knew if I ever said anything to anyone the physical abuse would become more severe. So, I buried all of my feelings, shed a whole lot of tears, lived in constant fear and kept quiet in order to appear normal. And, all the while I was dying a slow death because of the internal wounds of deep depression, loneliness and despair. I became a walking zombie harboring unwarranted emotions of guilt and shame as if I did something wrong. What a terrible and dreadful experience for a small child to endure. I repeatedly asked myself, "Who in their right mind would ever contemplate such cruelty against, not just their own child, but most notably—a child of God?"

My Father – My Nightmare

Normal, daily activities like bath time were not exactly a walk in the park for me. I didn't enjoy the fun, playful splash around time in the bathtub like most kids do—my father made sure he robbed me of this small but very endearing and amusing form of recreation as well. He would place me in the bathtub of scalding hot water and keep me there until my skin felt like it was on fire. Sometimes he would hold my head under the facet, face up, while I struggled to catch my breath. And just when I thought the nightmare was over and the pain couldn't get any worse—it did. He would use a cigarette lighter, hold it close to my skin near the bruises from the beatings, and literally watch my skin burn and blister. I can only recall two prevalent thoughts that consumed my mind during these awful, unbearable ordeals—how much I wanted to die and how much I wanted to see him dead.

Since the usual target areas my father chose to physically abuse were my chest, back, stomach and legs—I obviously couldn't wear shorts or take my shirt off like the other kids on the 90 degree summer days. It was years later before I figured out what my father's sick strategy was all about—to cover up the obvious. The visible marks and bruises on my legs, back and chest would explain the no shorts and leave the shirt on rule and most importantly, it would eliminate probing questions or inquiries from others.

I thought a father's ultimate role was to love his children and provide the highest level of guidance, training and support—not become their worst nightmare. Usually when a young boy thinks about his father, the tone of his mental and emotional being is most often with a respectful blend of positive admiration, excitement, and pride. Every child wants a father they can be proud of and most importantly, a father who loves them, a father who is wonderful and has devoted his life to protect and cherish them. When I think of my father my thoughts immediately shift toward the negative—mean, wicked, pathetic, cowardly, weak, insecure, empty and an imposter. He tortured everyone in the house in some way but my mother and I were his main targets. If my mother showed signs of affection toward me or tried to take up for me—she would get her lights completely knocked out.

Life is funny. My father is walking around today free as a bird, after doing these horrible, wretched things to me. He was never arrested nor charged even though the authorities knew (that's generally what happens in a small-minded, ignorant, backwards "Town of Mayberry" mindset. Yet, someone who commits tax evasion or uses dog fighting as a form of recreation spends years in prison. What a twisted society we live in. This is a man who desperately wanted the community to believe he was a good and decent Samaritan, a wonderful husband and father and a spiritually grounded man. Most definitely not true—all lies. Most people in the town eventually became aware of his mean spirited ways and angry outbursts. No one really liked him and made a point to stay away from him. He made my life a living hell and created a home environment that was precisely the same. Everyone in the household walked on egg shells. We were scared to say or do anything that may have upset him causing his volcanic personality to suddenly erupt. There were absolutely no happy times that I can recall while living with him, only misery. He made a point to always tell me that I wasn't worth anything, that I should have never been born. Just imagine how mentally damaging it is for a four year old child to hear these kinds of things his entire life, not understanding nor comprehending such negativity and hate. The mental and emotional effects were both traumatic and overwhelmingly destructive.

As a young child, I would watch the casual and intimate interaction between other boys and their father. I couldn't believe their connection—it had such a happy and natural flow. Not mine. It was the exact opposite. For years, I actually thought every boy endured the same ugly things from their fathers. What else could I have thought since that was all I ever knew or was exposed to. I don't have fond memories or fun recollections of any special times with my dad—every moment was tense, stressful and nerve-racking. And, every time I see this man or someone speaks his name—sad, vivid memories of what I experienced rises to the surface of my mind like molten lava. The mental snapshot I have of my life is nothing more than sheer, disgusting devastation. And all I wanted was to become invisible to the world so that I wouldn't have to talk or interact with anyone.

I always thought the love a father had for his son would be as easy and as natural as tying his shoes. I never considered the opposite. If only I knew why he was such an abusive man or why he didn't have the need to love me—maybe knowing would provide me with some sense of validation and as surprising as it may seem make me feel better.

Why couldn't I have a Father whose eyes lit up with excitement when I walked into a room or who showed genuine joy and happiness when we shared a special moment while watching a football game or playing Nintendo on a lazy summer afternoon. But instead, I had a father who tried to destroy me and was determined to hurt and abuse me in the same way he was abused. Yes, I believe my father was also a victim of child abuse. But instead of facing his own painful past and getting the help that he needed—he chose the cowardly, victimized route. He felt powerful and thrilled in releasing his extreme anxiety and anger onto me.

For years I struggled with the question—why me? Why did my father hate me so much? He had to hate me in order to do such terrible things, right? Obviously that's precisely how you think as a child. You don't have the educational comprehension or capacity to understand psychology and human behavior. The effects of my father's hatred unfortunately became an integral part of my adult life. He made me perform oral sex on him, masturbate him, as he sodomised me. I only knew that area as having one main function and how everyone cheered when it worked on the potty as expected. He made me feel ashamed, dirty and scared ALL THE TIME. How pathetically sad—a four year old who is barely old enough to tie his shoes, not having a clue as to what sodomy or any form of sex is, but yet expected to participate, keep quiet and cover up this sick secret for life. And if I cried, the beatings were that much worse. Yes, I was beyond sadness and depression—I was mentally, physically and emotionally immobilized. I didn't want to feel anymore, I didn't want to exist anymore, I just wanted to die.

Fortunately through counseling, I've learned how to cope and strive toward positive, healthy thinking and supportive people and things. But my father's demented survival strategies revealed his uncanny need to control and dominate me and others which in some peculiar way—made him feel better. But, all praise to God—I'm in control now. I am a grown man who struggled through the years of shame and hurt to finally connect with a life of routine and contentment. I made the decision years ago to cut off all contact with my father particularly during my healing phase. And, I really don't know if I'll ever be able to have a comfortable relationship with him. But right now, it's all about me and my peace of mind.

Why Me?

After twenty-two heart wrenching years, I still can't believe that this nightmare just won't go away. It continues to remain in the forefront of my mind repeatedly tormenting me with such sad and infuriating reminders of what happened to me for over nine long, exhausting years. Just imagine crying yourself to sleep every night for years and within a period of time, those painful tears turn into a raging anger causing your tearful nights to turn into sleepless ones. Trying to overcome and let go of the memory of a twisted world where secrets and sick rituals were part of my daily life has been an inconceivable and grueling process which has taken me what seems like an eternity to see my way through all of this.

As early as elementary school—I didn't have friends, no one to confide in and no one to come to my rescue. As far back as I can remember—I felt depressed, isolated and alone. Everyone thought I was weird or crazy. My mother as sweet and loving as she still is today—couldn't save me. She too was a victim of my father's abuse paralyzed with fear every time he walked into the room.

Most of my behavioral outburst began at school when my parents weren't around, during those times when I felt threatened or if a teacher/student were intentionally harassing me. I went through numerous counseling sessions with the school counselor and Psychiatrists but how could I possibly reveal to them what was happening to me. My father always insisted on being present at the counseling sessions. I was never allowed to speak with any of the counselors or doctors alone—my father was adamant about this request, everyone knew it and no one went against his demands. I knew better than open my mouth about anything my father was doing to me the consequences would have been dire. He would shoot me that evil, frightening look each and every time I was asked a question. But all I could do was shake with fear and remain tongue tied.

It seemed like getting into fights didn't phase me—I didn't care anymore because no one seemed to care about me. I became tired of being the victim and wanted others to hurt like I was hurting. After years of going back and forth to counseling sessions, doctor's offices and taking medications, the school's recommendation was to send me away to a residential treatment center at age 13. I was placed on heavy meds that kept me so drugged and lifeless I could barely think. And, this was their way of helping me—who figures? The principal of my high school told me that I was a menace to society.

I think I spent the first eighteen years of my life completely and totally mad at everyone. I was angry at my mother for not protecting me, I was angry with all of my teachers for judging me and punishing me instead of helping me. I was angry at the school system for not being more insightful in finding out what was really wrong with me. Instead they labeled me as an emotionally unstable, troubled youth who was in desperate need of serious counseling. My problem was not mental and there was no medication in the world that could cure my pain. My challenge was that I had been unjustly mistreated, forsaken by my father and forced at a young age to endure the impossible.

I've worked hard over the last five years to stay focused on self-improvement but I'm still human and I stumble from time to time. It seems like the moment I make some miraculous strides toward recovery and well on my way to a place of normalcy—out of the blue those haunting, unbearable memories of the past sadly penetrate their way back into my very guarded, personal space and I find myself reverting right back to those cheap feelings of shame and unworthiness. No one should have to live this way—dealing with the daily struggle of mere existence and fighting feverishly to release the guilt and humiliation that haunts my soul. I wake up hoping I can have just one day of welcomed peace. What's shocking is that something as simple as moving on with my life would be such a major undertaking. But it is. And, it has been throughout my adult life. I have a tendency to become easily upset about something or with someone all the time and all I want to do is punch someone's lights out, particularly those people who think they can say or do anything to me. My terrible temper is a work in progress. I will lash out at anyone who disrespects, embarrasses, or mistreats me. I refuse to endure any further abuse or unfair treatment in my life. I guess you could say I am my own advocate, fighting for continued survival and the three "P's" — Peace, Protection and Privacy. I learned a long time ago that I had to take care of me so that I could maintain my independence and assume all of the responsibility that goes along with being a grown up.

I don't blame myself anymore — I was only a baby when the incorrigible was happening to me. My life was turned upside down and inside out with terror, pain and fear. My little bit of joy and happiness were destroyed, my spirit was broken and my peace was stolen and taken away from me like a pathetic thief in the night and replaced with pointless, undeserved suffering. And to add insult to injury — no one ever came to save me. For over 9 years, I was forced to endure these unspeakable experiences, act normal, and pretend as if everything was okay. But trying to manage the unimaginable is not only irrational but virtually impossible — especially for a 4 year old kid. So, I did exactly what any child dealing with intense, emotional pain and trauma would do — I acted out in a major way. The truth is I was a ticking time bomb keeping everything bottled up inside with nothing to lose and ready to explode. And I did.

Kevin J? Welcome back

This is such a profound, realistic and truthful statement. There were far too many days that I honestly didn't think I would survive and would go crazy dealing with the constant struggle of just trying to forget.

What do you do when you've lost your faith, your hope and your will is gone? The answer didn't come to me overnight but now I know—you pray. And, you continue to stand strong and allow the Lord to get you through. I would be lying if I told you that all is well in my soul. I love the Lord. But I struggle every day with the realization that it's still so hard for me to trust. I'm holding on to my faith in God and his promise to never leave me nor forsaken me. And, He hasn't.

I made a conscious decision to give recognition to the Antoine Fisher poem because it was such an accurate reflection of my life. And, as an abused victim, I could relate to everything he went through. But in spite of the journey of neglect and abuse we both endured—we made the choice to persevere through courage and determination.

During my periods of depression, isolation and anger—I cry and often wonder, "what was wrong with me, why can't I rise above this thing?" I used to want to kill myself—to end the unbearable torment and suffering especially during those years when I was on an array of many anti-depressants and in and out of psych wards. And, the relationships I entered into were usually destructive. I always felt like I was going insane. Even today, I struggle with the conscious denial of the sexual and emotional abuse I endured as a boy. It is truly an intolerable curse to break.

But now I boldly recognize that I am a survivor of abuse. And if I hadn't received therapy, found a special female friend and recognized who was truly in control of my life—God—I would probably still be groping around in the darkness of my despair. Even while living with all the feelings of hurt and pain, I have worked hard to have a healthy life. At one time my focus was primarily on seeking revenge. I had this wide range of emotions and perceptions about my father, my abuser. But through the grace of God and the support of friends and family, I'm learning to pace myself and take one day at a time toward a journey of healing.

My message to anyone who has experienced a similar ordeal is to work hard every day to get your life back on track, in spite of your tragic past. I know how difficult it is to learn how to trust again and deal with all the after effects of abuse. You're left with such a deep, embedded sadness that never seems to go completely away. And those general clichés that people tell you to hold onto, "let go of the anger, forgive and forget, time will heal all wounds"—they're right. Store these positive affirmations into your mental computer so that you can grab onto them for strength and endurance.

The little boy in me still cries from time to time. I guess primarily because I'm still so confused as to why this happened. But, I'm pleased to say that through counseling, faith and emotional resolution —I survived. Each day brings about new challenges for me but it also presents another opportunity for my healing. Although I will never forget what happened during those years—let's just say that I'm glad to move on. Forgiveness is a special gift which requires a special process. I may never have an interest in reconnecting with my father but I thank God, friends and family who supported me and helped me through this horrible ordeal. And, I'm especially thankful to God for giving me the courage to tell my story in hopes of helping others in some special, uplifting way. I know now that I was not the cause of my abuse. It wasn't my fault, I didn't deserve it and, I was merely an innocent victim. But now, I'm a survivor—moving forward toward joy, peace and happiness.

Isaiah 41:10

So do not fear, for I am with you;
do not be dismayed, for I am your God.
I will strengthen you and help you;
I will uphold you with my righteous right hand.

I Won't Complain

"A Coal Miner's Courageous Journey"

Absolutely no one could have prepared my mother for the unimaginable, earth-shattering news she received on that cold and desolate night, February 18, 1955, in a small, coal mining town known as Cinderella, West Virginia. Why anyone would name a masculine coal mine Cinderella is beyond me but it became one of the longest lasting operations in the Williamson Coalfield, operating well into the 1970's.

Coal mining, in the state of West Virginia, played an integral role in the lives of so many men, especially African American men, and particularly during the 1940's, 50's and 60's – offering steady employment opportunities in spite of the low wages and perilous conditions. Nonetheless, the mines, nestled in a small, rustic, quaint community provided a means of survival along with a sense of fellowship and camaraderie for those seeking work and in search of a better life for themselves and their families.

My father, Manuel Reese Dodson, Sr., worked in the Cinderella Coal Mine for over 6 years laboring five days a week, sometimes six, in an effort to take care of his rapidly growing family. He was in the prime of his life – 30 years of age, full of extraordinary energy and determined to make a difference. But sometimes the unpredictable events of life can take a different turn contrary to one's respective ambitions and you find yourself in a vulnerable maze of unthinkable suffering and pain. That's exactly what happened to my father. His life plans were unexpectedly disrupted in spite of his goals and promising aspirations. Life decided to deal him a lousy hand of shattered despair when a huge boulder, while at work, fell from the ceiling of the mine shaft on top of him crushing his spinal cord and leaving him paralyzed from the waist down—depriving him of his God given ability to walk again. This dreadful truth happened over 60 years ago but to my mother, Mary Smith Dodson, it seemed like yesterday when the chilling, harsh reality of such a horrendous event knocked her into an oblivion state of emotional turmoil—forcing her to realize that the familiarity of her detailed and demanding life was about to change forever.

The Accident

It was around 8:00 pm—the house was peaceful and serene, very different from earlier that day when the atmosphere was filled with loud noises, constant chatter and fun filled activities of four small children (Manuel Jr., Paulette, Roland, Daniel). By now, all of my siblings were fast asleep, the youngest, Daniel, completely exhausted from the excitement of celebrating his first birthday. And for me—Sabrina Dodson, I was safely and securely tucked away in my mother's womb scheduled to be born three months later.

My dad was working his usual evening shift at the mines and my mother was casually engrossed in her daily routine of cleaning, picking up and preparing for bed. As she folded the last basket of clothes, she was startled by an alarming knock at the front door. Her first thought was that maybe one of the neighbors needed to borrow a cup of sugar or something of that sort. But then she wondered if something could be wrong because it was well after dinnertime and most of the women, at that time of night, were usually busy putting their children to bed and finishing up their last minute chores before going to bed themselves. Even the men went to bed early so that they could get up to tend to their chores before going to the mines. Slopping hogs, milking the cows and feeding the chickens were a common practice in the coal camp and most importantly, a reliable food source. Hard work was no stranger to this community. Each day required all hands on deck, children included, and without the benefit of modern technology and conveniences. Women didn't have the luxury of microwave ovens to warm a plate of food or a dishwasher to wash the pile of dishes dirtied throughout the day from a large family. Everyone stayed busy. So, it was a little unusual for folks to find the time to socialize in the late evening especially during the winter months when the bitter cold and darkness kept most people indoors.

After another loud knock at the door, my mother realized she had better answer it before the disturbing noise woke her children. She quickly made her way to the door and was solemnly greeted by two White men from the coal mining company standing on the front porch, obviously tense and nervous with the daunting task of delivering the bad news. She braced herself as one man handed her my Dad's mining cap and the other man handed her his lunch bucket as they proceeded to share the horrific details of his ill-fated accident. She'd heard stories of women whose husbands were either seriously injured or killed as a result of a coal mining tragedy, but she told herself not to think the worst and pray for a hopeful and encouraging report. "Your husband was in a serious accident and has been taken to the Williamson Memorial Hospital," stated one of the men. THAT WAS IT. Nothing else was said. There were no words of comfort, no compassion, no signs of empathy nor any considerate questions like, "Are you okay?" "Can we offer you a ride to the hospital?" "Is there anything we can do?" Both men walked off the porch and left. This was during an era when racism and segregation were real and quite prevalent. So, it was no surprise to think that these men were either too racist to care or too ignorant not to. My mother, in her frozen state of shock, ran to a friend's house to ask her to watch the children so she could rush to the hospital.

Upon arrival, the news about my father's prognosis was grave. The attending physician wasn't encouraging at all as he effortlessly informed my mother that my father wouldn't live through the night. He also stated that if by some miracle my father survived the night—the medical team would perform surgery the next morning to determine the extent of the damage. My mother's mental wheel began turning fast and hard. What did all this mean? What in the world will I do if my husband dies? How will I be able to provide for my children? She felt overwhelmed with fear. But in light of her panic-stricken anxiety she remained focused and prayerful. She directed all of her attention toward my father. She knew he was in shock although he managed to remain conscious and unbelievably calm. He didn't say very much, obviously struggling with the idea of how something this surreal could have happened to him. But there were no tears, no pity party and no cry for sympathy. My Dad was strong like that. He had that old school mentality whereas real men didn't cry. Men were required to act like men without showing outward signs of emotional weakness. And he lived by that standard until the day he died. But as amazingly strong as he was, I'm sure the words "Why me?" must've ran through his mind at some point that night. How could it not? He was lying in a hospital bed, paralyzed from the waist down and trying desperately to not only understand what had just happened to him but to find a way to grasp the distressing concept that he would never walk again nor perform the normal activities of his past life. But if this question ever entered his mind—he never once spoke it.

The one reflective comment my mother did recall my father saying as he laid obediently solemn in the hospital bed was "Take Care of the Children." A statement like that would lead one to believe that he thought he was going to die and the reality of managing life's responsibilities would be transferred to my mother. But that wasn't the case at all. He told me years later that he never once entertained the thought of dying nor did he feel any level of uncertainty within his spirit. He always knew that God spared his life for a reason and he was determined to fulfill his spiritual purpose along with his earthly responsibilities. Although, he did share with me that in spite of what he thought—his siblings and other family members were apparently thinking something different. Because they were consumed with worry and grief, their fragile, emotional state prompted them to gravitate toward the doctor's grim prognosis that he wouldn't live while my father's strong, unprecedented faith prompted him to gravitate toward God's prognosis that he would live. As expected, his brothers and sisters rushed to his side. Some of them lived in town—some of them lived out of town. And all of them remained steadfast and supportive at his bedside. But after a period of time, my Dad decided to deliver them from their mental anguish. He emphatically said, "Go back home, go back to work, you're losing money, I'm not going to die."

He was a Dodson—capable of enduring the inconceivable because of his family legacy of strength and perseverance. My father lived his entire life by this profound, deep rooted concept. My siblings and I heard the "You're a Dodson-You can do anything" speech at least a million times while growing up. Not to mention how he applied this teaching to practically everything he required or encouraged us to do. Whether it was going to the doctor to get a shot, having a tooth pulled, standing up to a bully, learning to ride a bicycle, trying out for the school band or speaking in front of the church congregation—we were always told if we demonstrated the highest level of courage, faith, and determination to succeed—we would because Dodson's didn't fail. The irony is that this encouraging idiom actually worked. We wanted so badly for our parents to be proud of us that we strived exceptionally hard to meet their expectations. And it helped us immensely throughout our lives to develop bold confidence and tenacity in our attempt to withstand life's challenges and sometimes cruel and painful moments.

The surgery lasted approximately ten hours and once again, the report was unfavorable—my father's spinal cord had been totally severed, cut in half and nothing could be done. He was paralyzed from the waist down, he would never walk again, he would never experience the joy of working outside the home, he would never experience a normal sex life, he would never play sports with his sons, he would never swim again and he would never walk his daughters down the aisle on their wedding day. And, to add insult to injury (literally)—the hospital's incompetent medical team put my father back to bed, allowed him to lie in the bed for over a month without any movement or rehabilitation and as a result, he developed chronic bed sores. Considering the fact that paraplegics have extremely poor circulation—it didn't take rocket science to figure out this was clearly the worst thing they could've done. The bed sores became acutely critical causing yet another grave concern.

During the 1950's, medical science was not particularly advanced in the area of spinal cord reconstruction not to mention that Williamson Memorial Hospital was the only medical facility in this small, underdeveloped town. But since my father miraculously survived the night of his accident and then forty or more nights thereafter—the doctors scratched their heads in amazement not comprehending this unexplainable miracle and not knowing exactly what to do with him. Finally, the decision was made to send him to the Crippled Children's Hospital in Orange, New Jersey to supposedly receive better care and aggressive rehabilitation—a hospital for children born without legs, arms, crippled or other major impairments.

This is where he was trained how to use his crutches to go up and down stairs, how to scoot, how to drive a car with hand controls, how to lift himself in and out of bed and how to use the toilet. And this is where he remained for the next eleven months—without his wife, without his family and without his friends. "Loneliness is the worst sickness in the world" is what my father used to say to my mother particularly when he felt the deep sadness and loneliness particularly on the weekends. This was generally the period of time when most of the patient's families would come to visit. My mother was only able to visit him five or six times within the eleven month period because the reality was that she was light years away in West Virginia taking care of five children and struggling to survive on limited funds.

My father didn't only lose his precious ability to walk after the coal mining accident—he lost his family health insurance benefits, life insurance and salary. The one saving grace was that he was able to go to any Veterans Hospital for medical care since he served in the United States Navy. Several months lapsed before a final decision was made to issue him an embarrassingly small, lifetime monthly annuity without insurance benefits. How ridiculously crazy was this? Not to mention the blatant unfairness of it all. My father had enough to deal with just trying to wrap his arms around the reality of paralysis and how he was going to make ends meet in order to provide housing, food, clothing, medical care and incidentals for a wife and five small children in the 1950's.

My father was now regarded as a paraplegic—wheelchair bound with limited capabilities and a discouraging future—a gloom and doom fate that would totally devastate the average man or woman to the point of chronic depression, emotional instability or death. But not my father—his spirited willpower and faithfulness knocked Mr. Dismal Destiny right out the ring. Remember—He's A Dodson. But most importantly, a child of our most high God whose word clearly states in Hebrews 13:5, "I will never leave you nor forsake you." My father knew without question that God spared his life for His purpose. So as any obedient Christian soldier would—he marched on with spiritual fortitude and resilience in his effort to endure the ultimate test.

It was well over a year before my father was able to return home to his family. And, upon his arrival, he laid eyes on me for the very first time since I hadn't been born when his accident occurred. I was 14 months old before my father was able to hold me. And I'm telling you it was truly love at first sight. My mother told me from that day forward I became his precious sidekick—following him around the house like a loyal, lost puppy. If he moved—I moved. She said I appeared totally in awe, mesmerized with his presence. I just wanted to be near my daddy. I honestly believe I was drawn to his strength even then.

There were so many changes my father had to make in his life after he returned home but he remained humble and amazingly independent. He refused to allow this setback to beat him or allow anyone to do anything for him that he could manage to do himself. But most importantly, he refused to accept mediocrity or shallow limitations for his life. This marked the beginning of my father's courageous journey and a testament of his remarkable power and unwavering commitment toward his spiritual purpose.

Who Was Manuel R. Dodson, Sr.?

Martin Luther King, Jr. said, "The ultimate measure of a man is not where he stands in moments of comfort and conveniences, but where he stands at times of challenge and controversy." Dr. King hit the nail right smack on the head with this quote because this is undeniably a direct and accurate reflection of my father's character and such an inspiration to all people who are faced with just a smidgen of adversity.

Manuel Reese Dodson, Sr. was born on December 1, 1924 in Gary, West Virginia, another small, coal mining town. He was the oldest son of George and Mary Dodson. At an early age, he accepted Jesus Christ as his Savior, was baptized and united with Bethlehem Baptist Church in Cinderella, WV. Immediately, after graduating from Aracoma High School in Logan, West Virginia, he enlisted in the United States Navy where he served three years as a Seaman First Class and received an Honorable Discharge in 1946. He attended West Virginia State College in Institute, West Virginia in 1947 where he received a Certificate of Proficiency in Electricity. While working in the Coal Mines he served as the President of the United Mine Workers (UMW) however, this prominent role was short lived due to a serious allegation that a group of racist white men were threatening to murder him for his unequivocal position on equality and justice for African American miners. This is exactly what happened to the first African American President of the UMW. He was shot down in the street like a defenseless dog. My paternal grandfather begged my father to step down knowing how serious this rumor was and didn't want my father to compromise his life.

My father accepted the call to become a Deacon of his church in 1952 and for many years, served as Chairman of the Deacon Board with a total of twelve deacons under his direction. He further served his community as a member of the Williamson Crown Lodge #16 (Mason), the NAACP, and the Mingo County Political League. During these years, my father was a catalyst for change which included facilitating integration of the school bus system and businesses in Williamson. It was in Williamson, West Virginia where he met and later married my mother, Mary Smith. They were married forty-nine years and from this union were born three sons, Manuel Jr., Roland, Daniel and two daughters, Paulette and Sabrina.

He was a distinguished, highly respected gentleman with extraordinary integrity, insurmountable strength and notable courage—a manly man, hard worker, serious minded, tough, honest, fearless and an advocate for equality. He believed that every individual had a spiritual, inherited purpose and how critical it was to discover it. He wasn't afraid of anything. And he was never apprehensive about speaking his mind yet he always did it with a fair and unbiased balance of finesse, tact and discretion. He was the backbone of our family—our mother was the heart. As much as he loved his children I think sometimes he thought we were part of his Navy Command. He ran a tight ship and there was never any question who was in charge. He didn't allow idleness—so looking busy was an essential part of growing up in our household. If you didn't look busy, he would definitely find something for you to do.

I saw my father accomplish ten times more from a wheelchair than an average, able-bodied man will do. Nothing went undone in our home. If my father couldn't fix something—he would call someone to do it. He had very little patience for underachievers, laziness or unmotivated souls. He believed in strong work ethics and honest accomplishments. My father's future may have seemed grim and discouraging to the rest of the world—but not to him. I use to observe the pitiful, gloomy faces of so many people as they watched him struggle as he lifted himself up the steps of our home, transfer from the car to his wheelchair or being carried into a building. I remember how amazed I was at my father's remarkable ability to respectfully acknowledge but at the same time graciously ignore the blank "I feel so sorry for you" stares of others and their sympathetic responses of compassion as they watched him trying to scoot on his crutches down the sidewalk silently praying that he didn't fall. But he understood. He never seemed bothered by what people thought nor did he allow their comments to influence his positive demeanor or mindset. He adjusted, he transformed and he recognized at the onset of his paralysis that this unjust setback was merely a faith driven setup for a spiritually compelled comeback. He would often say, "complaining doesn't change anything—faith changes everything". And that's precisely what kept him going—each and every day. On Sunday mornings everyone in our household was up and ready to attend Church Service—it was a requirement, not a request. My parent's spiritual principles were precisely the glue that kept our family strongly rooted in God's word.

Yes…You Can!

During the 2008 presidential campaign of our country's first African American President, Barack Obama—he chose a very simple, easy to remember slogan, "Yes, You Can". This slogan was obviously designed to be motivational yet it also had the ability to rouse voters to action. And, the most commendable aspect of Obama's "Yes We Can" slogan was its appeal to personal responsibility, not just in the political arena but in life.

My father, with his remarkable sense of courage and strength, was a testament to this basic, yet powerful life slogan. Despite the realization that he was a paraplegic for the last forty-three years of his life, he courageously assumed full responsibility to make his life worth living, to take care of his wife and children and to continue to honor, worship and demonstrate obedience to God for his unconditional love, mercy and grace. He had a myriad of hospital stays throughout his paralysis due to bed sores on his lower extremities caused by poor circulation. And these stays could last up to 8 months waiting for the sores to heal. And, if a skin graph was performed—it could take even longer. Four, five, six or eight months lying on your stomach, in the same position 24/7 is unimaginable to most but he did it patiently, obediently and without complaining.

Reflecting on the staggering years of his disability, my Dad could have opted to lie in bed wallowing in self-pity, advocating sympathy or, criticizing and accusing others for his predicament—he didn't. He could have chosen to embrace the "feel good" effects of narcotics or alcohol to numb the disturbing pain and despair—he didn't. He could have contemplated suicide in an effort to find a quick yet reckless release from life instead of having to endure the gloom and doom fate he had been given—he didn't. And, he could have denounced God as his personal savior, elected to gravitate toward anger and resentment, or question why God would allow something like this to happen to him—he didn't.

He chose a different way, God's way!

Life experiences, even tragedies, can make you stronger and in many instances—better. My father fought hard to sustain and live the life God planned for him and he did it faithfully. If God had a teacher's pet—it was Manuel Reese Dodson, Sr., if not for any other reason but the divine privilege and spiritual assignment he accepted in order to help a few special people along the way. He spent his life glorifying God and ministering to others to do the same. The most amazing part of his journey was the fact that he was able to do so many things that other people didn't think he could.

During the 50's and 60's, our country was not handicap accessible. There were no handicap accessible streets, ramps or elevators geared toward the convenience of the physically impaired. Although my father didn't work outside of the home to bring in extra money—he set up an electronic business in the garage of our home and repaired all types of electrical appliances. He drove the family car as an unofficial taxi in the community. He taught four out of five of his children to drive a car. He trained my brothers how to do anything related to basic maintenance and electricity. He taught all of us how to throw a baseball, bounce a basketball and survive. He attended the majority of the local high school basketball games in support of my cheerleading activities. He attended all five of his children's high school graduations. He attended our baptism and coached us in our spiritual walk. He helped us with our homework. He supported our dreams, always encouraging us to soar. Four out of five of us graduated from college. And, last but most definitely not least—he escorted my sister Paulette down the aisle on her wedding day. It may have been in his wheelchair but he did it—proudly, boldly and responsibly. My father beat all odds in regard to most paraplegics. And this was simply a tribute to his faithful, authentic spirit in

God's word. He was told that he wouldn't live through the night—he did. He was told that he wouldn't have a full life—he did. He was told that he would be limited to what he could do—he did whatever he set his mind to do. There may have been some changes in the quality of his life as it relates to his physical limitations but the incredible joy he experienced from the love and support of his family and friends was humbly cherished.

There are so many amputated souls in the world searching desperately for peace and understanding, particularly in the midst of a storm. But God's message to anyone who is lost and intently struggling to restore hopefulness and happiness back into their life—pray. If God be for us who can be against us? God will see you through the most perilous times. And all that is required—fall in love with Jesus, maintain your faith and continue to listen for that small, quiet voice of the Holy Spirit to lead, direct and guide you in in everything you do.

Was my father perfect? No. Did he have some good days? Yes. Did he have some weary days? Yes. Did he endure suffering during the forty-three years of his paralysis? Yes. Did he tire? Yes. But in spite of what he went through—*he never complained.* Always praise God—not just for what he's done but because of who He is. My father knew that his good days significantly outweighed his bad days because the Lord was always with him, blessing him with His favor.

My father's ability to endure and overcome the unforeseen obstacles and challenges of his life's journey inspired and uplifted so many people in our community. It was a testament in his spiritual charge to touch lives and make a difference. I know God was quite pleased with my Dad for always demonstrating an extraordinary level of agape love, kindness toward others and unselfish determination to share his divine wisdom and insight. He truly fulfilled his spiritual purpose. And when God was ready to bring my father, Manuel Reese Dodson, Sr. home, I strongly believe this is what He said, "Job Well Done You Good and Faithful Servant.

Thank you Lord for sharing with us such a Mighty Good Man!

Psalm 46: 1-3

1 God is our refuge and strength,
an ever-present help in trouble.
2 Therefore, we will not fear,
though the earth give way and the
mountains fall into the heart of the sea,
3 Though its waters road and foam and
the mountains quake with their surging.

"A Heart to Heart Talk with God"

On a warm, summer day in the Capital City... Washington, D.C., hundreds of residents and tourists alike bear witness to an unforgettable, extraordinary vision of physical excellence. In a flash...a bicycle zips by and you find yourself marveling at a picture-perfect image of total fitness meshed with the appearance of glistening tanned skin, beautiful white teeth and the most flawless, chiseled body only seen on a movie screen or an artists' canvas. "Is this a mirage?" so many have questioned, although residents have grown quite accustomed to the admiration and flattering stares aimed toward D.C. native, fitness guru...Stephen Hayes.

Stephen has respectfully earned the title of legend in the world of strength training with over forty years of fitness expertise, a consecutive winner of the capital area bodybuilding championship, fitness coach for Washington, D.C.'s former Mayors Sharon Pratt Kelly and the late Marion Barry, Jr., named in Vogue Magazine as one of the nation's top 55 Personal Fitness trainers in the country and his community advocacy to educate the young and enhance the mindset of the old on healthy living.

When Stephen isn't busy training a client or traveling the country to appear on radio/television shows promoting his health and fitness company, "The Hayes Way", an integral part of his fitness regimen is devoted toward spending time outdoors. He is either running the track at the University of Maryland, riding his bicycle through the parks and city streets of Washington, D.C. or making his way through the crowds at the annual fairs always humbly thankful for the opportunity to network and inform others on the importance of health and fitness.

For most people, maintaining a regular exercise routine or simply making a conscious decision to develop one can prove to be quite taxing not to mention the challenge and discipline it takes to advance into an effective workout program. Initially we all have good intentions working hard to adhere to our fitness goals and commitments primarily because we really do aspire to look good, feel good and do what's right for our body. But before we know it we find ourselves consumed with routine tasks, unwelcomed disruptions and more often than not—a major sense of failure.

But take a passion driven, motivated fitness expert like Stephen Hayes who has not only spent a lifetime building his fitness success but has earnestly and consistently practiced what he preached, dedicating an insurmountable level of time and effort to this fitness love affair.

Stephen does everything right when it comes to the preservation of his body—healthy eating habits, daily exercise, adequate rest, natural vitamins, conditioning, mental and spiritual meditation. He doesn't drink alcohol, he doesn't take drugs and he doesn't smoke—undoubtedly a specimen of unmitigated health and fitness. And as a veteran he has immersed himself in the subject of fitness spending hours researching new and improved methods of strength training as a means to cultivate physical awareness in his quest to address the health challenges of the community.

But despite Stephen's unwavering commitment to remain physically fit and impressively disciplined—the unexpected occurred. Without any warning an untimely and unwarranted event took place on Saturday, August 23, 2014 in Fort Myers, Florida. At approximately 7:00 pm, Stephen Hayes, a pillar of strength, a Hollywood head turner and a genuinely nice guy went into cardiac arrest while playing a video game with friends. His heart went into a deadly arrhythmia called Ventricular Fibrillation, described as a rhythm problem that occurs when the heart beats with rapid, erratic electrical impulses. When there is no electrical activity going on in the heart and the heart isn't beating correctly this will cause the heart to eventually stop—preventing oxygen from reaching the brain. And, when oxygen can't reach the brain, after a short period of time—the body will shut down. This is precisely what happened to Stephen—his heart just stopped beating.

What had appeared that morning as a seemingly quiet, relaxing day of fun and laughter suddenly turned into an atmosphere of sheer panic. While Stephen was playfully joking with his friends that he was unequivocally beating the pants off of them while playing one of their favorite games, it was at that very moment he fell to the floor. He didn't say anything, he didn't grab his chest, he didn't gasp for air...he simply blinked one time and he was out. By the grace of God his best friend reacted quickly and began performing CPR. He stated, "I honestly couldn't believe what was happening, the entire day was absolutely perfect—relaxation by the pool, light shopping and dinner without any warnings or signs of concern. Then within a miniscule second—I was frantically at work trying to save my friend. I never heard him say a word he just fell over."

Fifteen minutes had passed as Stephen's friends desperately awaited the arrival of the ambulance. But despite the fact that he had no heart rate, no blood pressure, no pulse—the CPR continued. They never gave up. Finally, the ambulance arrived and the paramedics worked feverishly to restore his heartbeat although initially they were unsuccessful. They tried the defibrillator. They administered Epinephrine, a drug used during CPR in hopes of reversing cardiac arrest. Finally a very slow, faint heartbeat was detected although Stephen remained unconscious. Immediately the paramedics strapped him onto the gurney and jetted out to the ambulance. But somewhere on the way to the hospital he stopped breathing once again. Stephen had flat-lined.

Urgently the medical team began working on him. Approximately 10 minutes had passed since he had stopped breathing so time was of the essence and all hope was beginning to fade. After continuous efforts they were finally successful in getting his heart started again. Once he was inside the hospital, the team of doctors continued to do everything medically possible to save his life by adhering to a variety of precautionary measures. A breathing machine, induced coma, lowered body temperature, heart monitor, intensive care were just a few of the measures taken to keep him alive, all along hoping for a favorable outcome. By the next morning the prognosis remained devastatingly grim. The doctors were just not optimistic. Stephen had gone without oxygen for well over 15 minutes and they were gravely concerned. But in spite of the grim prognosis the doctors did exactly what was required of them—they had to break the bad news to the family. Plain and simple they stated, "We don't expect Stephen to pull through. He may very possibly die at any time. And, if he does survive, there are a number of major concerns to consider". Will he wake up on his own or remain in a coma? Would he have extensive brain damage from loss of oxygen? What debilitating impact would it have on his neurological, cognitive and mental capacity? All these questions and more plagued their minds.

Stephen's six adult children had flown in from various parts of the country the next day after receiving the distressing news and all of them huddled in his room overwhelmed with fear. They couldn't imagine a world without their father. He had always been like a walking, talking fitness machine to them—teaching and validating the importance of health and fitness. Six out of eight of his children were high school and college athletes inheriting Stephen's physical attributes so they were all too familiar with the importance of maintaining a healthy physical regimen.

And most importantly, they exercised their faith, standing on God's word for His favor over their father's life. Based upon Stephen's prognosis, his children's spirits were declining rapidly causing them to feel useless and discouraged. All being saved—they understand the miraculous power of prayer. So, in spite of the unfavorable prognosis and the fact that their Dad remained in a coma—they knew the one and only answer to his recovery—God. They prayed, they cried and they believed. And most importantly, they exercised their faith, standing on God's word for His favor over their father's life. One of the doctor's on the team kindly had this to say to them, "If anyone can pull through this horrendous nightmare —this guy can. He is in excellent physical shape. I've never seen anyone his age in such tip top condition." What a sweet ray of hope his words gave them and suddenly a breeze of welcomed inspiration was blown into the room.

On the evening of the second day, the decision was made to slowly raise his body temperature in hopes that he would regain consciousness. This process would determine if there was any brain damage. Another day went by and he finally opened his eyes. This was a monumental step. Although Stephen was confused and disoriented—a miracle had just occurred. He was awake. This blessing marked the beginning of Stephen's incredible, faith based testimony to share with the world what God can do and the revelation of His unconditional love and wondrous power.

Do you recall the earlier statement regarding the doctor who shared his personal and professional insight that Stephen's physical condition would get him through? That doctor was precisely on point. He emphatically stated that all those years of Stephen's ability to maintain excellent physical fitness and discipline actually played a significant factor in saving his life.

An Intimate Conversation- by Stephen Hayes

I knocked on death's door on August 23,, 2014 and when He opened it—I was transformed. According to medical standards—I died. The paramedics were unable to detect any signs of life. And, during that long period of time when there was no sign of a pulse, no sign of a heartbeat, no blood pressure and no breathing—I was having a conversation with my deceased son, Antoine, on his birthday. This conversation was as real and as natural as if we were sitting at home watching a football game. But the most amazing and memorable part of this beautiful interaction was seeing the incredible, indescribable joy and happiness on his face. It glowed like a bright, shining star bursting with illuminating peace and serenity. Antoine always had a million dollar smile but this time his smile was different. It was infectious, like a magnetic, captivating force of love. I'd never seen him happier. We talked. We laughed. We joked. And then he placed his hand on my heart and said, "Everything is going to be alright Dad. Go back, it isn't your time". Of course I didn't know at that moment what had happened to me. I was just simply enjoying the conversation with my son. And all I knew was how much I wanted to stay with him, my oldest boy, who was tragically taken away from me at the young age of thirty-one.

God sent Antoine to have a heart to heart conversation with me. And, no one but God knew how desperately I needed that blessing to spend a little time with him. God knew the turmoil and sadness I've had for the thirteen years Antoine has been dead and most of all—how I've struggled with his death. I wanted to talk to my son again and I did. I wanted to experience that special bond that only a father and son can share—I did. I wanted to gaze into his eyes and allow my love for him to resonate—and, it did. Antoine touched and healed a part of my heart that has ached so deeply and for so long. Not one day has gone by that I don't think of him, miss him and regret all the wasted years we didn't take advantage of the time to hang out together. Life is unbelievably, unnervingly short. That's not a cliche'—it's the truth. And I can, without hesitation, attest to that realization.

No one could have convinced me that I would experience such an unfair and unforeseen ordeal. A cardiac arrest? Please...no possible way. How could something so disturbing and potentially damaging have happened to me? Everyone who knows me understands that exercise is my First, Middle and Last name. I live and breathe health and fitness. And, I am relentless in my pursuit to walk the talk.

When I started my personal fitness company over 20 years ago it was very clear to me that I needed to come up with a slogan that people could relate to—one that provided both authenticity and value toward their personal health goals and exercise schedule. The company's professional slogan, "A Healthy Body Enhances a Healthy Mind" has helped thousands of people become physically stronger and healthier. But more importantly, it has allowed me to advocate the fact that your body is your temple. It's your sole responsibility to do everything humanly possible to preserve it.

Nevertheless, after 40 years of daily trips to the gym yielding blood, sweat, no tears, but painful gain—an ordeal such as what I went through can still happen, to anyone. And in spite of this unsettling reality and my unshakeable faith—I still have that basic human need to ask, "Why Me?" "What did I do to deserve this?" "Was this some form of punishment?" or, "Was it simply my inability to recognize critical signs that something was wrong?"

Needless to say bad things happen all the time to good people. There was no way I could've predicted, prevented or prepared for this nightmare. It just happened. And, it happened to me. Out of nowhere, a miserable, dreary storm dangled its dark cloud of despair over my life as I laid defenseless in a hospital bed unknown to all if I would live or die. Imagine that? One moment you're walking, talking, laughing, and the next moment your heart stops beating. Nothing could be scarier. And to add insult to injury—the mystery of what caused the cardiac arrest still remains. Although numerous tests were conducted, the doctor's still don't know the actual cause.

Day 2

By the next morning the news about my ordeal had spread throughout DMV like wildfire. The love, support and prayers were pouring from every direction. And man did I need prayer—badly! The survival rate for someone in my condition was about 10 %. I'd say that's more than enough reason to be alarmed. So, it was going to take prayer and a miracle to save me. The next 48 hours were critical but friends and family remained faithful.

Day 3

Prayer truly works!

Waking up in a hospital room was indeed a new experience for me not to mention how surprised I was to see the array of machines and tubes running everywhere especially when I had absolutely no recollection of why I was there or what had happened. I was beyond groggy, weak and confused. All six of my adult children had flown in to be with me. And when I saw their faces my heart became overwhelmed with emotion. I cried. Not because of my current state but because I was so deeply touched by all of the love that filled that room. My three daughters were making over me as Daddy's little girls do—making me feel as special and as perfect as a newborn baby. My three sons demonstrated an impressive combination of resilience, compassion and sensitivity, all the while remaining steadfast and strong. I tried to speak but I couldn't. So, they filled in the blanks to all of the questions that were going through my mind, yet still focusing all of their attention in helping me to recover, recall and receive a general understanding of what was taking place. No one could ever know what that day meant to me having my children by my side. There are certainly no words meaningful enough to reflect my deepest, most intimate sentiments.

Day 4

The tubes are gone. The worried looks have lifted. I'm talking. And, finally some real food. Three days ago, no one believed I would pull through. But now, the progress has begun—slowly, carefully and joyfully.

It seemed like a busload of doctors, nurses and aides continued to come in and out of my room all day long—talking to me, examining me and scratching their heads in sheer amazement. Days after witnessing my astounding progress, several of the physicians and nursing staff shared with me that they had never seen such a miraculous event. I just smiled, looked to the Lord and once again said, Thank You. They said that I was the talk of the wing. Everyone wanted to check out the miracle guy in Room 1217. Apparently, the word around the hospital was…He's a 63 year old man with a body like a 30 year old and he survived the unimaginable. You would've thought I was a movie star with all of the attention I was getting. But only one thing resonated in my spirit—I'd been given a second chance at life, endorsed by our most gracious and merciful God, to fulfill a very special, spiritual purpose and to share with the world my incredible testimony. One thing I knew—I was not going to take this divine task lightly!

Only God

On the 11th day—I went through a myriad of test to determine if there was blockage in or around my heart—there wasn't. On the 12th day the medical team decided to insert a defibrillator in my heart. This was a precautionary measure as to jump start my heart, in the event that it stopped. Each day my mental and physical strength improved.

I spent a total of two weeks in the hospital before they would allow me to fly home to DMV. But that was okay because I knew I needed the time to heal. Since my return, I've had several medical appointments along with an array of tests. This has been a long and tedious journey. And, it's been particularly challenging for me because my daily regimen for over 50 years consisted of exercise and sports. However, I give thanks to God each day for a new day with improved health and progress. I'm doing just fine.

I talk to God all the time. I actually have a heart to heart talk with him every day, all day. It's because of Him that I can share this miraculous story. It's my unprecedented love for God and faith in His word that helps me move forward and live life the way God intends us to. And, even though I felt all of this before my ordeal—my relationship with Him now is so intimate and fulfilling.

It feels different as if I'm talking to my best friend, my spiritual confidante, my unchanging savior.

My touch with death brought me closer to God. I thought this setback was the darkest hour of my life, unfair even, but in essence it has turned out to be my brightest hour. I wouldn't be alive today if God hadn't afforded me another opportunity to fulfill my spiritual purpose and to make some things right. I no longer take life, family or friends for granted. I appreciate the blessing of another day. This experience has aroused a part of me that was numb and unfamiliar. A part that was not always open to spiritual change and restoration. But I got it now. I see the big picture. I see how God works and how he uses each of us as vessels to help, inspire and save others. Absolutely nothing could feel any better. I don't cling to the past anymore, I only welcome the future. I celebrate each day for God's favor and give sincere thanks for the blessings in my life. During the healing process, I had a lot of time to think and reflect on my life—things I did well and the things I didn't. During those long periods of enforced reflection, it became especially clear how to separate the important from the trivial, the worthwhile from the waste. My hunger for spiritual knowledge immediately replaced my hunger for insignificant things.

Life is funny. We spend a lifetime working hard to acquire all the pleasures of life, grasping for that little piece of happiness, comfort, financial security and love. And all of these things are important. They are aligned with God's word. But just remember to always place God first and foremost in your life and all the little pieces of what we're trying to achieve will fall right into place.

I truly love the Lord and I want to tell everyone how wonderful and merciful God is and that He will never leave you nor forsaken you as long as you believe in Him and have faith in His word. You don't have to worry nor have any fear—God will supply all of your needs and take care of you. I'm sure most people have either gone through or going through something in their life that has made them feel disheartened and confused. Stay encouraged. Never lose sight of the kind of God we serve—loving, wonderful, comforting and everlasting.

Since my ordeal, I no longer have a fear of death. But I did. And, if we're all totally honest—who doesn't? It's an unknown entity that no one can actually tell us the specific details of transitioning. But I don't feel that way anymore. When I saw the sweet joy and peace on my son Antoine's face while talking to him—my fear of death has vanished completely. This is not to say that I'm ready to go to my heavenly home now. It simply means that when God is ready to bring me home after I've accomplished what He has instructed me to do—I will be ready—willfully and obediently. Love others, never waiver in your Faith and know that God is always in control.

Psalm 25:5

Guide me in your truth and teach me,
for you are God my Savior,
and my hope is in you all day long.

Amazing Grace

"Amazing Grace" is undoubtedly the most recognized and favorite gospel hymn of all time primarily because of its remarkable melody and ever-popular narrative of personal redemption.

On June 17, 2015, President Barack Obama delivered a heartfelt eulogy at the funeral of the prominent Reverend Clementa Pinckney, Senior Pastor of Mother Emanuel A.M.E. Church in Charleston, South Carolina, who was one of nine persons gunned down by a racist terrorist during Bible Study. But as prevailing and moving as Obama's message was—absolutely no one will ever forget how he graciously commenced into a solo of Amazing Grace bringing a church full of mourners to their feet filling them with astounding inspiration and encouragement as they sang along.

So what makes this song so admired and so powerful? I think most believers would agree that it's not necessarily the music itself but that the power of the song is in the lyrics which are totally reflective of God's grace.

Amazing grace! How sweet the sound,
That saved a wretch like me!
I once was lost but now am found,
Was blind, but now I see.
T'was grace that taught my heart to fear.
And grace, my fears relieved;
How precious did that grace appear

The hour I first believed!

God loves us. And because He loves us so much He gives us mercy and grace. While the terms have similar meanings—they are not the same. Mercy is deliverance from judgment. Simply meaning—God not punishing us as our sins deserve. Grace, an undeserved kindness, an unmerited favor, is God blessing us despite the fact that we do not deserve it. This is merely an extension of His kindness to the unworthy, providing extraordinary, divine assistance needed to carry us through those moments of difficulty, distress, doubt or sorrow.

So. If God grants mercy to deliver us from our transgressions and grace to weather the storms which essentially help us in the moments we find our faith lacking—then why the constant fear and frustration? Why do we repeatedly question our trials and tribulations? Why do we think our current or past offenses warrant punishment from God?

Sadly enough, there are far too many Christians that think their sins are justification for their suffering. A close friend of mine "Jessie" believed just that. And he shared this disturbing sentiment with me during one of our visits as he laid helplessly stricken with A.L.S. (Amyotrophic Lateral Sclerosis), a rapidly progressive fatal neurological disease that attacks the nerve cells responsible for controlling voluntary muscles. In short, this disease weakens muscle control and gravely deteriorates total physical function. A.L.S. is a thief that robs you of your fundamental ability to walk, function and live. And, to add insult to injury—there's no known cure.

What conceivably happened to bring about such an unexplainable and unexpected illness on Jessie—a vibrant, energetic young man of 59 years of age who spent every day tirelessly helping others and desperately striving to live a purpose driven life. Could it have been the result of an unfortunate accident he endured as a child at the young age of three when he fell down a flight of concrete stairs hitting his head causing a mild concussion and severe lacerations? Could it have been the time he was brutally attacked in his mid-thirties by several men who imposed critical blows to his head leaving him for dead? Or, could it have been a myriad of old football head injuries that went untreated possibly causing irreparable damage?

No one, including medical science, really knows if any of these incidents played an integral part in Jessie's demise. And because there isn't a cure or treatment that can neither stop nor reverse ALS, scientists remain at a loss. Although, medical professionals do have a better understanding regarding the make-up of the disease based upon an article printed in the Journal of Neuropathology and Experimental Neurology which stated the following, "studies have proven that repetitive head trauma resulting from collision sports such as football and boxing may be associated with a motor neuron disease that is similar to, yet distinct from, ALS."

For months even before Jessie's diagnosis, he experienced severe, excruciating pain in his back and legs. He was told that this problem was the result of damaged nerve endings in the vertebrae (old athlete's injury) that would require surgery in order to repair. Jessie realized he had two options—to continue in his current state or, take a chance with surgery in hopes of restoring his life back to normal. He definitely wasn't thrilled at the idea of surgery but because the pain became intensely worse as each day passed—he opted for the surgery.

I'm sure most people cringe at the thought of spine surgery clearly because it scares the living daylights out of them not to mention the horror stories people share on how they were worse off after the surgery than before. But all Jessie wanted was to experience a pain free, healthy lifestyle and once again have the ability to manage something as effortlessly as walking. Yet the thought of family and friends taking time out of their busy schedule to care for him was probably more unsettling to Jessie than the surgery itself. He was always known to be an independent, self-sufficient and prideful man who never wanted to be a burden to anyone even though he was always so appreciative of those who shared their love and support.

The surgery was over and Jessie could finally embrace the reality of a successful recovery. He was pleased that he remained diligent in his daily exercises and determined to struggle through rehab within the anticipated timeframe. But instead of his workouts becoming easier, they became increasingly harder. On some days it was virtually impossible to get through one simple exercise. Even though Jessie had been told that physical therapy could be painfully grueling in the beginning he felt something was off. He detected a level of discomfort that was strangely unfamiliar than anything he'd experienced before the surgery. Initially he chalked it up as a sign of age and the fact that he hadn't been able to work out like he used to and desperately needed to get back into the gym. But in his spirit he knew something was wrong—terribly wrong.

Days turned into weeks with very little improvement in his progress causing Jessie and his therapist to become gravely concerned. He wasn't making the leaps and bounds expected—actually, not even close. So his doctor ordered additional test in hopes of identifying the problem. He told Jessie to remain patient and he would contact him as soon as the results came in.

After a few days, Jessie began feeling anxious. He hated the idea of waiting for an answer to such an unusual situation mainly because no one had a clue what was wrong. Not knowing what was happening to his body caused more of a mental and physical strain on him than the problem itself.

Finally, Jessie received a call to meet with his physician. Overwhelmed with nervousness he braced himself as the doctor reluctantly delivered the dreadful news. "Jessie you have A.L.S." Complete silence entered the room. It wasn't that J. didn't know what A.L.S. was—he knew exactly what it was but painfully trying to wrap his mind around this unsettling news. Another pinched nerve perhaps? But the Big A? No Cure? Even cancer, commonly known as the "Big C" with advanced drugs and new medical procedures has given so many people a positive sense of hope of being cured. There had to be some kind of mistake. This nightmare just couldn't be happening to him. Only a month ago, he was told that surgery and rehab would fix him right up.

After several minutes of intense meditation coupled with the struggle of processing what was just told to him—the reality that he had been misdiagnosed finally hit home. Jessie's thoughts quickly reverted to all those months of thinking he had a pinched nerve. He never imagined that all the time he spent mentally preparing for major surgery, building stamina to get through a brutal regimen of therapy and trying desperately to bear an unexplained level of pain and discomfort was all futile.

Jessie had been given a prognosis that was not only irresponsible, careless and wrong—it was unacceptable. He was led to believe that there was a chance to restore normalcy to his life through surgery, determination and confidence. Although millions of lives are cured and saved everyday by the advancement of medical science—it's still emotionally devastating when they're wrong.

There were no words to accurately describe Jessie's state of mind. Depression, sadness, anger, resentment and fear were all valid emotions churning around in his spirit, frantically trying to identify something good out of a hopeless situation.

As Jessie sat in silence waiting for his sister to pick him up from the hospital he began asking himself, over and over again, "Why me?" "What could I have possibly done to deserve such a horrendous fate?" "Is this my punishment?" "Is this how I will die?"

Jessie's Story

Jessie passed away two years ago. But approximately one month before he transitioned, I visited him. He had been transported to a well-known effective rehabilitation center for continued treatment. During our visit, I immediately noticed the difficulty he had talking and his shortness of breath was painfully obvious. We spent about 30 minutes talking about the details of his condition and the progress he'd made although he anxiously wanted to share a personal story with me in spite of his struggle to talk—a life changing event that took place when he was about 45 years of age. He spoke about how God's amazing grace saved him and all the while provided spiritual clarity and purpose to his life. As stated previously, Jessie believed that some of the things he had done earlier in his life was primarily the reason he was suffering through this ordeal.

During a telephone conversation I had with Jessie shortly after his surgery(before he found out he had A.L.S.), I mentioned to him that I was writing a spiritual self-help book. I provided him with a brief synopsis and he seemed quite interested. He conveyed to me that he too had planned to write a book about his life and asked me if I would help. Although several weeks later is when he found out he had A.L.S. It was at that time he asked if I would write his story to include in my book. Without hesitation, I said, "yes".

The following story is written in first person which are "Jessie's" personal sentiments.

"God's miraculous grace changed me but most importantly, saved my life". I experienced an amazing yet unusual epiphany on one of the lowest days of my life. Never in my wildest dreams did I imagine that a person's soul could actually shed tears. Mine did. My spirit was beyond desolation forcing me to sink deeper and deeper into a pit of despair. I just didn't know this kind of sadness and hopelessness existed. I was mentally defeated, emotionally barren, spiritually despondent, agitated, scared and losing my mind trying to make sense of a dire situation that I'd carelessly fallen into. Call it reap what you sow, reckless behavior or just good old fashion bad luck. All I knew was that I needed a major plan of "help me get out of this mess" and a hand full of prayer warriors to intercede—quick, fast and in a hurry.

I was facing 20 years in federal prison for tax evasion and a few other charges they were trying to pin on me. I'd spent well over 15 years building my empire of worldly possessions acquiring everything I wanted from money, businesses, beautiful women, cars, houses and things. I was totally driven to get all that I could get. For years I felt on top of the world with the monetary success I'd always dreamed and I worked hard to get there.

Life's funny—because while you're busy getting all you can get you never really stop to think about the possibility of losing it or being in a position to see it all come crashing down at the blink of an eye. Well—without warning, my empire began to crumble. I was faced with major IRS issues, dishonest business partners, unfavorable street hustlers and terrified that I may go to jail. After a couple meetings with federal prosecutors who had made it very clear to me what I was up against—reality set in and I knew I had major trouble.

In my alone time, I began reminiscing about my life choices, my dreams, my goals and the detrimental twist and turns I experienced to achieve all that I had. As wonderful and satisfying it is to have money in your life—sometimes it can become a bad omen especially depending on how it came about and the people you dealt with to get it. I thought about my childhood, all the fond memories and the invaluable moral and spiritual guidance I received from my mother and grandmother. I thought to myself, "what would they tell me to do?"

When I was about 25 years of age, my evangelist grandmother asked me to pick her up so that she could go to the grocery store and run a few errands which is something we typically did on Saturdays. I always enjoyed spending that special time with my grandmother and truly valued the wisdom and spiritual insight she shared with me. She was unquestionably the matriarch of our family and everyone knew it. She was an exceptionally strong woman, faithful and fully committed to doing

God's work each and every day. And she didn't play when it came to demonstrating spiritual integrity, faith and respect toward others.

After we'd made a few stops and were heading down Florida Avenue in Washington, D.C. I noticed a drunkard urinating on the street in broad daylight. He was relatively tall, slim statue, brown complexion, around thirtyish and noticeably inebriated. Pointing at him, I said with astonishment, "Grandma, look at that man peeing on the street for everyone to see". My Grandma turned to look and immediately told me to stop the car. Surprised, I said "stop the car—why"? "Boy, do what I tell you, stop the car—I want to talk to that young man" she said. "Grandma, you can't go over there and talk to a drunk. He may attack you or something. I can't let you do that". "Son, stay in the car and wait for me, I got this". I watched my grandma get out of the car with such bold confidence and spiritual fortitude. Her faithful spirit was always reflective in her daily walk. Out of concern for my grandma's safety, I continued to watch the man as she calmly and assertively strolled over to him, began talking to him and before I knew it, she laid hands on him and began to pray. I mean she prayed a fervent prayer over his life, a sinner's prayer, a heart-felt prayer most pleasing to God. After about 20 minutes, she got back into the car and graciously told me to drive on—her work was done. She told me that as a missionary our job is to help others, uplift spirits and save souls and to always remember that at any time an opportunity presents itself to do God's work—you do it. She told me that you don't know a person's background, what they've been exposed to or how they ended up where they are. Our job is to love and support, not to judge. I was absolutely stunned at what I'd just witnessed. I was blessed to be a part of something uniquely special that had taken place on that day.

So here I am—twenty years later trying to figure out how my life hit rock bottom. And, I honestly couldn't see any way out. I began to think horrible thoughts. I wanted to be free from all of this trouble and free from pain. It was a Fall afternoon and after things had calmed down from a busy workday and all the staff had gone home—I stepped outside my office which had a separate exit to the back of the building. I sat down on the steps and starred at the sky for what seemed like hours. The longer I sat the harder I stressed and the heavier my spirit began to feel. Finally, without warning, my head just hung down low, my shoulders followed suit aching with agony—and my body began to shake intensely as I sobbed uncontrollably. I prayed hard asking and pleading with God to help me, to give me another chance to turn my life around and only glorify Him, not money, not things—only Him. I prayed to God that if He helped me out of this mess, I would give my life to him fully and completely. I would spend the rest of my life being His vessel to minister and save souls. I don't know how long I was outside crying—I actually lost track of time but all of a sudden I felt a strong yet comforting grip on my shoulder. Who in the world is touching me, I thought. I didn't hear anyone come out of the warehouse nor did I see anyone walk pass me. Then a powerful, reassuring voice said to me, "God loves you and everything is going to be okay". I quickly turned around, blinked my teary eyes in an effort to focus and see who was behind this caring, compassionate voice. Lo and behold I realized I knew that face, I'd seen that man before. I kept thinking, who is this man and where did he come from? After seconds passed my mind kept turning over and over to place where I knew this man. Finally I thought—it can't possibly be who I think it is—no possible way. The man standing over me comforting me, reassuring me, uplifting me was the same man, the drunkard that my grandmother prayed for and saved from a life of sin, homelessness and brokenness on a street corner—20 years ago. He told me that after my grandmother did what she did for him—his life began to change almost immediately. He was now a minister, had his own church and was saving souls everyday—just like my grandma did for him. He and I talked for a long while and I shared with him what I was going through. He prayed with me and told me about the goodness of the Lord and how He would get me through this terrible situation—to completely align my life to God's work, have unshakeable faith and continue being obedient to God's word. I did. The obstacles I was facing began to miraculously fade away slowly but surely because of God's amazing grace. Doors that were closed began to open which allowed me to resolve many of my issues. I gave my life completely to God just like I promised. I couldn't wait to get to church on Sundays to give God all the praise. I joined the church choir, I became a member of the men's ministry and I served on the usher board. Whatever I felt within my spirit to do for God—I did it.

Obedience became my best friend although it isn't easy. Sometimes we want things to go our way and not God's way. And, when things don't go like we want, when someone says something unbecoming to us or rubs us the wrong way, when our difficulties and circumstances overconsume us—"we get angry, irritated, we don't like it". Now here's the real rub: Just because we are living a life of obedience doesn't auto-magically make our situation better, it doesn't mean we become pain and trouble free. A lot of believers think that by being obedient all of our problems will just go away whether it's health issues, marital problems, financial challenges, addictions or unemployment. Things happen…but God is always good. And, as long as we submit to the will of God in our daily walk, and our prayer-life, we can sustain the painful times. I'm just so happy to share with everyone that God saved a wretch like me!

"Amazing Grace….that saved a wretch like me."

Aren't we glad that grace saves us in spite of our wretched ways? No one wants to admit how wretched they are—it's so much easier to live in the self-delusion that compared to others we aren't all that bad. But the harsh reality is that we've all fallen short of God's glory.

The term "wretch" simply means deviant, damned, worldly, foolish, disobedient, morally and spiritually corrupt. These terms, at one time or other, have applied to essentially all of us particularly in our younger years when it was so tempting to yield to the forbidden pleasures of the world. But, lo and behold divine intervention occurs and our spirits willfully succumb to spiritual discernment prompting us to tap into our faithfulness. This phenomenal awakening most often occurs as a result of a major tragedy or trial in our life encouraging us to call upon the name of Jesus to save us from a self-absorbed world of despair. That's called an epiphany—a sudden realization about the meaning of something i.e. the meaning of your life and what direction you're heading in.

Amazing grace is the love of Jesus whose agonizing death and victorious resurrection saves us from who we really are—not from who we think we are. When you can honestly say that His grace saved a wretch like you, you can begin to stand in amazement at the greatness of His grace.

In memory of my good friend Jessie, a loyal, obedient and faithful child of a most high God—I honor him by using the acronym A.L.S. to define his true, authentic character...*Amazingly Loyal Soldier.* He lived to serve God in whatever way would be pleasing and honorable to Him. And Jessie understood that God allows things to happen according to His sovereign plan. He prepared himself for his day of transition and he passed away with a peaceful spirit in a room filled with indescribable love from family and friends.

Is there life after failure?—Yes. Because of God's amazing grace, all things are possible.

Deuteronomy 31:8

"The LORD is the one who goes ahead of you; He will be with you.
He will not fail you or forsake you.
Do not fear or be dismayed."

Beauty Is Only Skin Deep

"Vitiligo – A Silent Sadness"

My sister and I attended a play at the Arena Stage in Washington, D.C. with our Sunday Brunch Book Club several years ago and after a very enjoyable afternoon we walked back to our car only to realize it wouldn't start. It appeared that the battery was dead as a result of leaving one of the car doors partially open for over three hours. Nevertheless, we called AAA and within 30 minutes the technician arrived. He called to let me know that he was parked in front of the Arena Stage but didn't see me. I'd given the AAA Customer Service Representative a description of my car along with the address of the facility but then I realized I was actually parked on the side of the building. I told the Technician to drive approximately 300 feet around the bend and he would see me standing outside a Silver Nissan Murano waving my hand. I stayed on the phone with him as he proceeded enroute and in my effort to assist him in my identification – I told him I was African American with light brown hair, wearing a black and gold jacket. Within seconds I spotted his truck. I began to wave anxiously and asked him did he see me? He laughed and said in a very amusing but respectful manner, "Yes Ms. Hayes – I see you!" I wasn't quite sure where the humor was coming from but as I watched him park his truck the thought of what he was laughing about finally resonated. To him, I wasn't Black—at least not by the color of my skin. It was at that very moment the harsh reality that my skin color had changed dramatically finally hit home. I was no longer the brown sugar baby my momma gave birth to. *Bummer.*

Over 85% of my natural brown color has turned milky white due to Vitiligo, an autoimmune disease I was diagnosed with over twenty years ago. Yet, for years I still envisioned myself as having brown skin. But in spite of this cosmetic nightmare, my race, heritage, ancestry, culture, and consciousness has not changed. I know who I am—a resilient, humble and confident child of the Most High God. I made up my mind at the onset of receiving this unfavorable news that I wouldn't allow this horrible affliction beat me nor alter my faith. I decided to persevere in my quest to demonstrate unspeakable strength as I prepared to embrace this spiritual journey. I've been tasked with the responsibility to reveal God's goodness in spite of my trial. And, I graciously accepted this charge in an effort to help others embrace their test, endure the painful moments and elevate toward victory, not defeat.

The technician was still chuckling as he approached me, staring at my face and not quite sure what to make of what I had just told him. The funny part—I wasn't offended. I'd become accustomed to the myriad of confused looks and stares, ignorant gawking and the pathetic expressions on the faces of others usually clueless as to why this severe discoloration was so prevalent on my face and body. I couldn't begin to tell you the number of questions that go through my mind each time I see someone looking at me. Do I look scary? Are the spots actually worse than I imagined? Should I stay in the house and never come out? Am I an embarrassment to my family and friends? How do others deal with this unsettling reality? Will I ever look normal again? Will I be able to live with this cosmetic nightmare?

I'm one of the fortunate ones—I was able to come to peace with this unsolicited ordeal many years ago. I merely had two choices: stick my head in the sand like an ostrich—avoiding people and social contacts or, stand strong and become a beacon of light for others going through something similar. I gladly chose the latter. What would it say about my faith if I bowed out of the race and allowed a skin disorder to defeat me?

After conducting extensive research on the disease, I realized that many of the questions swirling through my mind are essentially characteristic of a person suffering from Vitiligo. And yes, Vitiligo patients suffer terribly. It's an indescribable, deep-rooted sadness that consumes your mental and emotional state of mind. Yet you fight hard to silence your true feelings so others won't pity you. But don't get it twisted, it's hard as the dickens not to let it bother you. Who wants to feel physically inadequate? No one. It's absolutely humiliating, awkward and embarrassing—not to mention, exhausting. And your social life is greatly impacted as well. Not many men or women are secure enough to date someone with the disease—they can't handle the peculiarity associated with Vitiligo.

I met a man on an online dating service years ago and after several months of talking on the telephone we decided to meet at a public place. Immediately, I saw the look of disappointment in his eyes as soon as he saw me. He did however manage to maintain his composure for the next two hours we spent talking. Needless to say that relationship didn't blossom and, he had the audacity to call me several times alluding to only one thing which I wasn't having. I'm nobody's party girl or charity case.

Dealing with Vitiligo is not in any way easy or painless. You're constantly trying to find creative ways to escape the unwanted attention and annoying stares. When you walk into a public place—you sometimes hold your head down, intentionally avoiding eye contact because you're just not up for the all eyes on you saga nor the unwanted reactions. All you hope for is that this awful nightmare will end—somehow, someway. And just maybe if you blink your eyes, your natural color will miraculously reappear. But unfortunately, it's just not that simple. There are no known cures for Vitiligo—only treatments and to add insult to injury—the treatments aren't successful for all patients. Trying to process and merely comprehend the diagnosis that your natural born color will eventually disappear is beyond discouraging. But most people find a way to accept the fact that there's not a darn thing you can do about it. What worked for me was prayer, prayer, prayer. Let's not forget about the children. Over 2 million Americans have Vitiligo and 50% are children and teens. And these precious babies are tormented by the constant stares, name calling, teasing and bullying by other children and sometimes even ostracized. Look into the eyes of a child with Vitiligo and I guarantee you will see the silent sadness and pain. It's just heartbreaking to know how cruel people can be, both children and adults. Some people believe it's contagious and refuse to have any physical contact with persons with Vitiligo. I believe that adults should know better, although many are uneducated about Vitiligo, and children are oblivious, fearful and don't understand.

Vitiligo is an extremely stressful disorder and affects one's emotional being. A bad sunburn and severe stress have been known to provoke the onset or progression of the disease. Ninety percent of dermatologists say to patients, "It doesn't kill you, just go home and don't worry about it." Chances are—not one of these dermatologist have Vitiligo. Therefore, as the saying goes, "until you walk in my shoes...". Another scary reality is that there's no way to predict how this disease will progress from one patient to another. It truly takes a form of it's own. It can begin on the face of one patient but nowhere else on the body or spots begin to surface all over the body of another patient slowly and continuous. And it doesn't only affect skin color but hair, the inside of the mouth and even the eyes. Normally, the color of hair, skin and eyes is determined by melanin and vitiligo occurs when the cells that produce melanin die or stop functioning. But the uplifting news is that it's not life-threatening or contagious. The treatments that are available for vitiligo may improve the appearance of the skin but it does not cure the disease. People with the disease must be vigilant about using sunscreen with a high sun protection factor on the body parts with white spots year-round especially while in the sun and should wear long sleeves, pants and wide-brimmed hats. I went to St. Johns, Virgin Island about three years after I was diagnosed with Vitiligo and a large part of my lower arms were mostly white. I laid out on the beach even though it wasn't particularly hot that day but the sun rays were strong. I didn't use sunscreen and I couldn't believe how my skin immediately blistered after about an hour. That scared me silly and straight. Moving forward, I adhered to the medical advice to always cover up and use plenty of sunscreen in spite of how long I spend in the sun. Your skin is definitely exposed—there's no protective covering.

Pushing through the painful moments of discomfort, depression, embarrassment and shame is just part of the course and most people find the strength and capacity to deal with it. My journey with Vitiligo has been consistently challenging because of the rapid progression of pigmentation loss. On one particular week, I would see a conglomerate of small light spots that would gradually pop up on my hands, arms, legs or stomach then out of nowhere large white patches would appear the next week or so. It was quite alarming when the spots began appearing on my face. But it wasn't always the disease that caused me the most pain. People did. I get it—the fact that the peculiarity of its appearance may cause the rubberneck ogling and insensitive glares. But, let's not forget those special persons who are scared silly that just by shaking your hand they will most likely catch it. That's just plain old ignorance. It really hurts me to say this but on several occasions I'd detected a slight hesitation from people who didn't want to shake my hand or someone sitting beside me in church when instructed to hold my hand during prayer or benediction. They didn't appear too happy. These are God fearing, Bible toting, Love the Lord church people I'm talking about. But I guess if you don't know better—you can't possibly behave better. Then you have those inquisitive souls who dare to ask the unwelcomed questions such as, "What happened to your skin?", "Were you burned?", "Are those spots on your face a birthmark?" or, "Doesn't it bother you when people stare?" And, I want so badly to say to them, "What do you think?"

Nevertheless I don't and I won't.

Bottom line—it takes a mighty strong spirit to manage the ignorance of others. So, if I'm able to educate others—I don't mind sharing the gory details of my struggle. Unbeknownst to me, there are still a number of people (black people) who aren't familiar with the disease. Didn't they know about Michael Jackson? He most definitely had Vitiligo. And, this is precisely why he slowly but surely turned from Black to White. He did however go through a treatment process that helped speed up the melanin loss in order to become one color because I'm sure most, if not all Vitiligo patients will agree that after dealing with black and white spots all over your body—you'd rather be one color. But a few side effects of this treatment is that the eyes become extremely sensitive to light and the loss of melanin can never be restored.

Now for me—I opted to *let it do what it do* because it would be my luck that the moment I decided to go through the treatment is when the medical profession would find a cure. Call me chicken but I love my black skin and would like nothing more than another opportunity to see it again. I'm happy that there aren't many black spots remaining although the larger ones are most prevalent on my face. Now, I'm forced to use heavy makeup on my face but not my entire body. The light concealer and powders help to cover up the dark spots and the bronze and dark brown powder help to give me a little color. This helps to avoid the blotchy, uneven look. Some days it really doesn't look all that bad. And then on other days, it looks downright strange. I can usually tell when my makeup is blending well or not, by the expressions on people's faces. They stare especially hard when my makeup skills apparently need some work. If I don't get an over-abundance of stares—then I know I was successful in the right application. What's really crazy is trying to keep the makeup from getting on everything and it's a monster trying to get it out of my clothes and furniture. The makeup seems to get on my car seats, steering wheel, door, dashboard, visor and basically everything at home and work...on the doorknobs, light switches, doorways, keyboard and desk because there's always a mild residue that seems to remain on my hands in spite of how much I wash them. I have to dry clean my suits and jackets after one wear because the makeup gets on the collar since I have to apply the makeup on my neck to blend with my face. And what I hate the most is when people lean over to give me a kiss on the cheek, they come back up with white lips or white makeup on their nose and/or cheek. I try hard now to let people know in advance to avoid touching my face with theirs. It's so embarrassing!

I remember like yesterday when I received the disturbing news that I had Vitiligo. This was a disease that I had gravely feared since childhood. I was terrified the first time I saw a young man around 20 years of age at a church revival with the disease. He was a tall, attractive man with a dark chocolate skin tone and an infectious smile that could light up a room. Yet, the large, discolored white spots on his face were practically screaming for attention—drawing all eyes toward this bizarre condition. I was seven years of age during this time and I immediately prayed, "God please don't let this awful, scary looking thing happen to me." Little did I know—it would. I don't think I saw anyone else with Vitiligo until I went off to college about ten years later and once I did, I had the same reaction—sheer panic. I grew up in a small coal mining town in West Virginia where Blacks made up about one percent of the population. I suppose this was partly the reason I didn't know much about Vitiligo. Although I don't think anyone did. But I learned much later that it can affect any race, although it's not as noticeable in white people or those with lighter complexions. But the disturbing reality is that each time I witnessed someone with Vitiligo—I felt an instant uneasiness in my stomach. Each time I was just trying to comprehend how anyone could manage something so surreal—an unpredictable event that can change your entire physical appearance forever causing an insurmountable degree of pain and suffering along the way.

I was about 43 years old when I received my diagnosis. My skin tone was a medium brown and I always went to great lengths to ensure my physical appearance was reflective of the way my mother trained me—a presentation of elegance, respect and style. Now this statement is not in anyway an indication of conceit or arrogance but simply a strong dose of good old fashion home training coupled with engrained humility, pride and self-respect. I grew up in an era where image and presentation was an important factor in who you were and even a greater reflection of your parents. You were taught to care about how you looked each and every time you left the house which simply meant well-groomed hair, makeup, clothes, shoes, accessories all had a proper and perfect place in your overall presentation.

The first noticeable sign of Vitiligo on my body alarmed me greatly. I was getting ready for work and observed these small, white spots on my right breast and arm. I sat down on the edge of my bed and thought, "Oh my Lord, it can't be—all awhile praying it wasn't what I thought". I kept telling myself not to think the worse and to just wait and see if they would go away. My family and I had just returned from a vacation at the beach and were sporting some pretty dark suntans so I figured that had something to do with the spots. But after a couple of weeks and the spots remained—I made an appointment with my primary care physician. Upon examining me, he was hesitant in his diagnosis because he really wasn't sure what caused the spots so he referred me to a Dermatologist who confirmed immediately that it was Vitiligo. He was candid but polite as he proceeded to tell me what I was up against. There was no known cure for Vitiligo but a few available treatments that proved successful for some patients but not for all. He also shared how the disease can be very progressive in for some while others may see a few contained spots. Murphy's law—I had the progressive kind. With each passing year, my natural color began to disappear. It was a cosmetic nightmare.

Why did this happen to me? How could a skin disorder I had essentially feared for years just slide into my life? I couldn't help but think I'd done something wrong and that this horrible skin disease just happened to be my punishment. Why me, Lord? Is this my test to justify my eternal love for you and my obedience to your word? Will this be a significant part of my testimony to help save and strengthen others who may be going through a similar ordeal? Am I strong enough to endure the emotional pain and discomfort? I was making myself miserable trying to make sense of all of this. Then... immediate peace resonated within my spirit. I knew the answers even before I asked the questions. WHY ME is not the question. WHY NOT ME is the ultimate response. Who did I think I was questioning God as to why He would allow such a thing to happen to me? Why would I fathom, even for a second, that I was too good, too holy or too faithful to endure such a test? Didn't I know that everything is about God's glory and His purpose? My job was to obey, endure and take the test.

I don't talk about the disease much with family and friends primarily because it's my spiritual assignment—not theirs. And, I didn't want to cloud my perspective or disrupt my focus with outside comments and opinions. I didn't want to see faces of pity. I've always been viewed as an emotionally strong woman, trained by my parents not to showcase your weaknesses but to elevate your strengths. Therefore, I was determined to manage this task with God's help and not burden those who loved me most. And more importantly demonstrate God's eternal love and favor through this journey to afford others the privilege to witness miraculous power.

Now, it would be remiss of me to pretend as if this test has been a breeze and that I've gotten through the past 20 years unscathed. The truth? I don't like it at all. I've had some pretty low days as a result of dealing with this chapter of my life. There were times I didn't have the emotional strength to get out of bed much less go to work or outside the house. What can I say—I'm human. This unfavorable challenge actually zaps you of your positive energy and self-worth replacing it with unhappiness and despair. For years I realized I was in a whirlwind ordeal, constantly battling unwanted spots and struggling to hide them. But each and every day God gave me the strength to persevere, shake off the pity party blues and keep it moving. And I did. But I really think it's important to point out to those who have fallen down due to some unexpected, unforeseen tragedy or occurrence in their life to know that anything shocking or upsetting is painful and it takes time to restore and repair. When the spots on my face were popping up like popcorn and making me feel like a circus clown, I endured a great deal of stress trying to figure out how to cover up the spots. My profession requires interacting with people all day, every day so naturally I'm always interested in looking my best 100% of the time. Because I tried for so long to maintain my brown skin tone by using darker makeup—I finally accepted the fact that it wasn't working. I had a brown face and a white neck—crazy. I just didn't know how to transition to all white and I didn't want to. I spoke to several Black Cosmetologists knowing they would be able to hook me up—nope. Didn't happen. They appeared about as clueless as I was which is still quite surprising to me. Most of them told me to check out Fashion Fair cosmetics which sold makeup specifically for chronic skin conditions like Vitiligo. I did, but none of the technicians offered assistance in how to apply it. Finally, after several years—I received a referral to a Mac Cosmetologist who could help me. And she did. The amazing part was that she was White and more willing to help me than the Black ladies. She spent well over two hours teaching me how to apply the makeup to reduce the splotchy, uneven look and how to lighten the dark spots and blend with the white. I was more than grateful so she received a $40.00 tip that day which was—my pleasure. Thank God for the invention of makeup and for blessing me with that young lady's compassionate spirit and kindness.

Back to my story. After years of painfully watching a few spots turn into a multitude of mountainous large white patches, it became even harder to accept the realization that my physical appearance had become unfamiliar, indeed an unwelcomed transformation. I began to question how this would affect my social life. Would a man be attracted to me? What about his confidence? Would he be strong enough to manage the stares and stress associated with this skin disorder?

Normally I wouldn't dream of going out of the house without first applying my makeup – but there's always a first time. Not to mention that it takes at least 45 minutes to put it on perfectly. Anyway – one Saturday morning I needed to go to the grocery store, run a few errands and I was pressed for time so I may a conscious decision to not put on any makeup. I thought to myself, "This is who I am. I shouldn't be ashamed. It's time for me to deal with the general public's reaction". Well I did just that and let me tell you it was a true eye opener for me. I saw looks of pity, shock, fear, sadness and shame. I wish I could say that it didn't bother me – but it did. And I get it. When people witness anything unusual or peculiar it draws a lot of attention and it's hard for people to mask their reaction especially when they don't have a clue what it is. Needless to say – I didn't try that performance again. Way too distressing. But like so many others with the disease I find myself from time to time looking at old pictures, reminiscing about my appearance especially in my adolescent and young adult life and thinking about the attention and notoriety I received primarily because of what some may say – my beauty.

I fondly remember a story my mother repeatedly shared with me reaching back to the day I was born. The nurses on the maternity ward of the hospital decided to take me around the various floors showing me off to various patients because they thought I was such a beautiful black baby – to the point that my mother had to ask where I was!

Remember this was in the 1950's so we all know nothing as remotely as this would ever occur in today's society. I always enjoyed hearing this story because it made me feel happy and special. But, aren't all babies beautiful not to mention divinely special? At least I've always thought so. I suspect that this transient event was the starting point of the myriad of compliments I most humbly received in my life through a variety of settings, circumstances and experiences. I had the privilege of being the first African American Cheerleader and Homecoming Queen in the history of my high school; I participated in a number of beauty pageants in my community and in the State of West Virginia. Once I moved to the Washington, D.C. area, I became a runway model and appeared in several reputable magazines modeling hair products and even on a couple of television programs. But my story isn't about accolades, compliments or even baby stardom but merely about the realization that physical beauty, in spite of its diverse quality of distinctiveness and admiration can vanish without a moment's notice for any reason.

Someone once said, "Physical beauty is superficial and is not as important as a person's intellectual, emotional and spiritual qualities." Well if this is indeed a true statement—then why all the fuss? In this country, Americans alone spend billions of dollars every year trying desperately to look and feel a certain way. Bigger lips, butts, breast, nose jobs, etc. has become an integral part of our society to look our best and better than the rest. And, as sadly as it is known—it's usually not so much of wanting to, but pressured to. We all want so badly to be accepted by society's idealistic standards of image and personality that we continuously strive hard to remain trendy and fashionable to the point of radical exhaustion.

What does the Bible say about Beauty and Outward Appearance?

Proverbs 31:30: "Charm is deceptive, and beauty is fleeting; but a woman who fears the LORD is to be praised."

What it means: "Beauty fades with age, so if you are more concerned with your outer appearance, you will be unhappy when the wrinkles come and the number on the scale goes up. In fact, did you know that your body may show the beginning signs of aging as early as age twenty? That is why God wants us to "fear" Him. That doesn't mean to be afraid of Him but rather to be in awe of Him and all that He has done. Let me put it to you this way. If you stand two girls next to each other and one is Miss Teen USA whose beauty is limited to physical beauty, and the other young lady is a more average-looking girl who loves the Lord more than anything, she is the more beautiful girl in the eyes of God."

1 Timothy 4:8: "Physical exercise has some value, but spiritual exercise is much more important, for it promises a reward in both this life and the next."

What it means: "Exercising and staying in shape is a good thing, but God expects us to stay in shape spiritually by reading our Bibles, praying, and going to church on a regular basis. In other words, there will be plenty of people who put their time and effort into staying in shape but who are out of shape spiritually. If they don't know

Jesus Christ, their perfect bodies won't get them through the gates of heaven."

1 Samuel 16:7: "But the LORD said to Samuel, "Do not consider his appearance or his height, for I have rejected him. The LORD does not look at the things man looks at. Man looks at the outward appearance, but the LORD looks at the heart."

What it means: "The world focuses on what people look like on the outside. God focuses on what people look like on the inside. Do you put more time and effort into being pretty on the outside or the inside? While there's nothing wrong with wanting to look pretty, we need to make sure it's in balance. God would rather see us work on becoming drop-dead gorgeous on the inside. You know, the kind of girl who talks to Him on a regular basis (prayer) and reads her Bible.

The Holy Spirit led me to share my personal testimony in hopes of helping others manage their spiritual journey whatever the trial or test. Everything you endure is all part of God's purpose for your life, helping you to understand how all the pieces fit together and most importantly, experiencing the incredible sense of hope, energy, and joy that comes from discovering why God designed you, what you're destined to do, and receiving the discipline required to prepare you for eternity. I've struggled for years to manage the uncontrollable variables of dealing with Vitiligo but God kept me and He has given me incredible strength, peace and a perpetual attitude to worship Him and glorify His presence all the time. I'm especially grateful that my journey has been a blessing to others, that I didn't keep my head buried in the sand but persevered with confidence and self-pride. Years ago, a young man in his mid-twenties, began working in my office—he too has Vitiligo. He shared with me after spending several years at the company how much he appreciated and admired my faith and confidence in managing the disease. He said by watching me appear unharmed nor impacted by this crazy, unexplainable condition gave him new found courage and helped him to overcome the shame and emotional despair he'd felt for so many years. The Holy Spirit quickens you, heals the body, comforts the mind and gives you a calmness that comes out of nowhere when you're dealing with adversity. You just have to learn to appreciate God's goodness, move forward with a strong sense of fortitude and faith, pray consistently and thank God every day for absolutely everything. Remember, He is not punishing you but preparing you for divine disruption".

Romans 12:12

Be joyful in hope, patient in affliction,
faithful in prayer.

PART 3:

CONCLUSION

Why Me? Why Not Me?

Most of us could not begin to entertain the despairing thought of our lives being sadly altered or shattered as a result of an unfair, unforeseen trial, obstacle or tragedy. Just think about the hundreds of things that can actually happen to you or someone you love. An explosion disfigures the face and body of a young man; an eighteen year old boy loses his life in combat; a fire takes the lives of three family members; a couple loses their only son to the horrific carelessness of a drunk driver; a teenage girl is found mutilated and buried in the woods; an infant is born blind; a mother of four is diagnosed with AIDS; a young boy is fatally wounded while walking home from school; a 10 year old commits suicide from bullying; a child is reported missing; a young girl becomes the victim of sex trafficking; a father murders his two small children and takes his own life; a young girl is diagnosed with brain cancer; a married couple lose their jobs, their home and custody of their children; a natural disaster destroys thousands of homes and all of it's possessions.

Tragedies like these happen every day—and no matter how hard we try to refrain from these unpleasant, dreadful thoughts—no one is exempt. I think Forrest Gump said it best, "Life is like a box of chocolates—you never know what you are going to get". Although this statement comes directly from a movie and most likely perceived as a relatively simple statement—it still conveys an insightful message regarding the heightened level of anxiety people have about the unanticipated, surprising events that can occur. No one has the capacity to foresee or escape the bizarre incidents that could occur in their lives—in spite of their fundamental level of intellect. There is no way we would ever know the kind of hand we'll be dealt in life. One precious moment you are loving and living your life to the fullest; experiencing an abundance of sheer joy and happiness; truly valuing all that you have been blessed with—a great job, ideal partner, good health, obedient children, wonderful marriage, successful business, supportive family and friends, financial security, beautiful home, material possessions and most of all, peace of mind. And, within a minuscule split of that precious moment—everything that you are most comfortable with—everything that is completely familiar and natural to you—what's certain, what's real, what's true—can change. The unimaginable happens and you find yourself in the midst of a storm.

Can you remember a time when something inconceivable happened to you? How did you handle it? Did you blame God? Did you lose trust in God and begin to question your faith? Did you become angry and bitter? Did you place unwarranted fault on others? How did you manage day to day living? Did you feel the pressure to pretend as if everything was okay? Did you begin to feel as if life wasn't worth living? Did you want to die? Did your mind scream, Why Me? Did you feel as if God was punishing you? Did you feel as if God had forsaken you?

These are basic questions that enter our minds when something bad happens. If you are one of those people who continuously struggle to understand why these terrible things happen—stop. You will drive yourself absolutely crazy trying to come up with some logical or acceptable rationale. No one can make sense of evil. And, you can't blame God. He is not the one punishing you or causing you the pain. But here you are—faced with adversity, faced with a test of your faith, and forced to decide how YOU are going to handle it. We begin to question our spiritual allegiance, racking our minds with various thoughts such as....Did I sin against God? Did I intentionally offend someone? Have I been selfish? Am I ungrateful? Did I betray a friend's trust? Do I intentionally mistreat people? Have I been disobedient? Did I refuse to honor a harmless request from someone because I was tired? Did I neglect my responsibilities in giving money to a friend in need? Could it have been the fact that I'm having an affair with my best friend's husband? Is it because I spread gossip and tell lies? Was it because I haven't attended church within the last year? Is it because I don't tithe? Is it because I cheated on my taxes? Could it have been the time the cashier gave me too much in change and I didn't say anything? Is it because I neglect my responsibility to help my sick mother?

Rather than beat yourself up, day after day, trying desperately to find an answer to nothing more than a self absorbed question—fight your battle of adversity with radical, spiritual fortitude and not concentrate on the empathetic question of Why Me?

The question of Why Me basically infers that one's focus is on the problem and not the deliverance. And what's most important is to believe in God's promise. When you find yourself in an unfortunate situation you can't understand, don't question "Why Me?" Simply ask yourself, "Why Not Me?" As a child of God, your spiritual stamina and determination can withstand any test, trial or tribulation because of your faith in God. All you have to do is lift up your head and hands unto the Lord, pray for strength and surrender all unto Him. He will always take care of you—just ask.

Find Purpose and Joy In Your Life

In the midst of a personal storm, when your soul becomes exhausted and heavily infected with jaded, cynical thoughts—that's the ideal time to praise God. When everything is going great how can you see the goodness of the Lord?

You may not always have the human capacity to do something that could change your situation but you *can* have a victorious outcome—through faith and perseverance. Despite our failures and their consequences, God gives us hope and His mere presence and favor is available for all of us to experience. Our job is to remain steadfast through the storm and allow the Holy Spirit to equip us, empower us and embolden us so that we will have the supernatural power to handle it, go through it and survive it.

The devil wants you to lose hope but most of all, lose your faith. Don't ever let him prevail, and he won't—because God's love never fails. God will not leave or forsaken His children. Many of us have gone through an unfortunate experience as either the victim of a tragedy or traumatized by a tragic event that violated a family member or close friend. And, it's difficult to handle. Remember, God's will is not always the easiest road but through faith—God will get you through the storm, all you have to do is ask Him to help you. God makes a way when there seems to be no way.

James 1:12 says, *"Blessed is the man who remains steadfast under trial, for when he has stood the test he will receive the crown of life, which God has promised to those who love him.*

Romans 8:28 says, *"We know that God causes all things to work together for good to those who love God, to those who are called according to His purpose."*

Proverbs 3:5 says, *"Trust in the Lord with all your heart and lean not on your own understanding"*.

These scriptures give hope and meaning in spite of one's grave circumstances. Believe in God's promise wholeheartedly and do it without doubt, fear or distrust and victory shall be yours.

You know you serve an awesome God and that the word of God is our number one spiritual weapon.

When you are hurting deeply and there's a wound in your emotions—God can heal it. We are basically powerless in our capacity to comprehend and explain why painful events occur. But through eradication, we learn how to stand firm in our faith and demonstrate goodness and compassion in our desire to help one another.

In your prayer time, ask God to use you as a vessel to fortify spirits of pain, abuse and oppression. Your experiences, your testimony and your life can have a significant impact in changing a hopeless soul to a hopeful one.

APPENDIX I:

A Tribute to the Lonely

A Tribute to the Lonely

Now if there's a smile on my face
It's only there trying to fool the public
But don't let my glad expression
Give you the wrong impression
'Cause really I'm sad, Oh I'm sadder than sad
But ain't too much sadder than
The tears of a clown when there's no one around

-Smokey Robinson

Loneliness is a sad, tragic reality…an utterly empty shell of existence.

Do you know someone who is dreadfully lonely, sad or depressed? Have you or do you know of someone who've experienced the excruciating pain of losing or watching a young child die a slow death and, the shallow emptiness and misery they feel every day—all day? Are you aware that millions of people, young and old, wake up each day totally alone without a soul to love them, care for them or save them? Can you imagine having to find fun and joy in a tedious task such as going to the grocery store or walking around the mall just to be around people? What about the sweet, innocent children? The forgotten one's who were rejected, abused or forced into foster care yet desperately yearning for the love and comforting arms of their mother or a sweet, compassionate surrogate. If you know someone who's harboring desperation or, unfamiliar with God's word that "He can do all things for those who love the Lord" – have you done all you can do to embrace their sadness, lift their spirits, and provide helpful resources and kind words of encouragement?

I often ask myself, "How can people be so lonely when they *appear* to be so happy?" Are people *not* as transparent as we think? Why can't we detect the obvious signs of loneliness and sadness in our personal relationships with friends, family and coworkers? Shouldn't we know the normal behaviors of the people closest to us? How do we lose the connection of what's really going on with them or ignore the warning signs that something's terribly wrong? Is it that we're just too absorbed and preoccupied with our own lives? Do we even care or try to understand? Or, is it simply our inability to demonstrate vigilance to what's real and what's not?

I strongly believe that the lyrics above accurately reflect the undetected agony of so many. Why? Because a smile can be unquestionably deceiving giving the impression of happiness. And behind that fake, masked smile where the hidden origin of pain dwells – the lonely tears flow triggering despair and endless hopelessness.

This tribute is to sincerely and prayerfully acknowledge all the lonely hearts and souls striving frantically to find a sense of peace and reconnect to that one positive, uplifting emotion we call *happiness*.

Usually we regard loneliness as an enemy because heartache is definitely not something we choose to invite in. Loneliness, a silent plague and one of the last taboos, is a hot topic in this country even though most people don't like talking about it because they feel others will laugh or judge them for not having friends or a close family. Some might even think it's stupid or childish to admit they're lonely. But the reality is that loneliness can happen to any of us at any time, for any reason. So…for the lost souls who are unable to envision hopefulness beyond their loneliness I wish to convey this message – you're *not* alone. Learn how to fight the burden of loneliness through prayer and look to God for continuous comfort and strength. Ask God to send someone to your life as an authentic, endlessly supportive friend who can inspire you and help you find that perfect balance of peace and joy.

Can you imagine anyone who would voluntarily choose to be alienated, alone or disconnected from everyone? Just think about the hollowness a person experiences when there are…No friends or family to check on you; No friends to hang out with at school; No friends to share your highs and lows or those extra special moments; No companion or spouse to hold, comfort and love you through your pain; No desire to live after the death of a spouse, child or best friend; No mother or father to support and guide you through your struggles; No confidante to help you manage and navigate through the enormous pressures and responsibilities of a demanding career, health issues or the physical and financial accountability of taking care of elderly parents.

What about the long list of married people who are just as lonely, if not more, than single people? They too suffer – *severely*. And it's usually a combination of either battling a strong divide with a spouse or being married to someone who just doesn't know how to express or demonstrate their love.

Another key concern in our country is our youth. Everyday more and more young people are seeking counseling to help them deal with low self-esteem, loneliness and depression. They're trying desperately to achieve a perfect fit in an imperfect world due to constant pressures such as cyber-bullying, social media and peer hassles. All of this along with being faced with the pressure of keeping up with the expectations of friends, struggling to cope with the anxiety of what other people think and being constantly bullied creates a lack of confidence, worthlessness and a nation full of deeply unhappy children which can lead to drugs, chronic depression or suicide which is sometimes demonstrated through an horrific social media trend of livestreaming.

Years ago, my sister worked as Director of Social Services at a nursing home in the DMV area. She shared several stories with me in regard to the loneliness that far too many elderly people experience due to several unfortunate factors. Some outlive their spouse, friends and in many instances their child(ren); some never married; some may have been an only child meaning there were no nieces or nephews; some had parents who were an only child; and, some distanced themselves from family and friends. The point is...many of our seniors have absolutely no visitors, no advocates—*no love*. What a horribly upsetting and unimaginable concept particularly to people fortunate enough to have a relatively large family and a whole host of friends. Knowing there are people who are merely existing and totally alone without one caring person in this big old crazy world to visit them and love them is truly a heartbreaking reality.

Loneliness tends to be a strange affliction causing us to be a bit scared and fearful of being alone or not being loved, needed or cared about. But so many people are reluctant to confide in others about what they're going through. There's absolutely nothing wrong with sharing your feelings in an effort to feel better. Why can't we trust more so that we can triumph when the powerful hearts and minds of others encourage us—helping us to rise up with confidence, spiritual fortitude and faith?

Research reveals that nearly one in five Americans suffer from chronic loneliness and that everyone will experience feelings of loneliness at some point in their lives. According to research of Nicholas Epley, Assistant Professor of Behavioral Science at the University of Chicago, "loneliness is a greater risk for mortality than cigarette smoking, can cause major health concerns and possibly increase a person's chance of premature death by 14 percent". Psychological studies have also shown that in order to have true happiness in life—most people need at least one close friend.

If you're blessed to have a life of busy, plenty of friends and family who love you—consider taking the high road for a change and make time for those who don't. Support the lonely, pray for those sad, broken hearts of despair and include them in your life. Invite them to your home when you have a family dinner; remember their birthday and do something extra special; make a concerted effort to call and check on them; request the names of the sick and shut-in at your church and surprise them with a thoughtful gift of love. Let them know you're genuinely concerned and available if needed. Isn't our ultimate spiritual task to help and uplift broken spirits? So... if you've ever felt loneliness, even for a brief moment, hopefully this message has helped you to gain a greater sense of compassion and empathy.

As we are all aware...a clown's role is to make everyone happy with a smile painted on his face. But like others battling with sadness—*he cries too.* It's always important to remember that even though you're feeling happiness and contentment in your life, there are many others who aren't. Please look for that ideal opportunity to extend a special kindness and agape love to others every day—all day.

"the true measure of friendship isn't how you feel about someone else – it's about how they make you feel about yourself"

Author Unknown

APPENDIX II:

Discussion Questions

Discussion QUESTIONS

The following discussion questions can be used in your small group, book club or Sunday school class.

1. Can you think of a experience you've encountered that could help others who are going through the same kind of situation? What major source of advice would you provide to help comfort and encourage them?

2. How helpful do you find this book as it applies to difficult and distressing ordeals in your own life?

3. Do you believe Christians have the capacity to endure trials and tribulations easier than non-Christians? If yes…why? If no....why not?

4. After reading this book, what lesson(s) have you learned? Has it broadened your perspective in how to manage a difficult issue or tragedy of some kind?

5. Which testimony affected you the most? Explain why.

6. What helpful recommendations can you provide to someone going through a similar ordeal such as "Kevin"-Who Will Cry? or "Jessie"-Amazing Grace?

7. Was there something especially uplifting or motivating about one of the testimonies? If so, which one and why?

8. Which of the five personal testimonies resonated the most with you? Which story seemed relevant to either a past or current experience? Explain why.

9. After reading the testimony, "I Won't Complain-Manuel" which of the following words best describe your sentiments e.g. encouraged, compassionate, angry, sad, hopeful?

10. In your opinion, what was the author's main objective in writing this book (e.g. to teach, uplift, motivate, bring light to a dark, hopeless situation)?

Made in the USA
Monee, IL
06 July 2024